Better Homes and Gardens

Christmas

101 WONDROUS IDEAS

Better Homes and Gardens® Books
Des Moines, Iowa

Better Homes and Gardens® Books
An Imprint of Meredith® Books

christmas

Editor: Carol Field Dahlstrom
Technical Editor: Susan M. Banker
Graphic Designer: Angela Haupert Hoogensen
Copy Chief: Terri Fredrickson
Managers, Book Production: Pam Kvitne,
    Marjorie J. Schenkelberg
Contributing Copy Editor: Arianna McKinney
Contributing Proofreaders: Karen Grossman,
    Colleen Johnson, Elizabeth White
Technical Illustrator: Chris Neubauer Graphics, Inc.
Electronic Production Coordinator: Paula Forest
Editorial and Design Assistants: Judy Bailey,
    Mary Lee Gavin, Karen Schirm

Meredith® Books
Editor in Chief: James D. Blume
Design Director: Matt Strelecki
Managing Editor: Gregory H. Kayko

Director, Retail Sales and Marketing: Terry Unsworth
Director, Sales, Special Markets: Rita McMullen
Director, Sales, Premiums: Michael A. Peterson
Director, Sales, Retail: Tom Wierzbicki
Director, Book Marketing: Brad Elmitt
Director, Operations: George A. Susral
Director, Production: Douglas M. Johnston

Vice President, General Manager: Jamie L. Martin

Better Homes and Gardens® Magazine
Editor in Chief: Jean LemMon
Executive Food Editor: Nancy Byal

Meredith Publishing Group
President, Publishing Group: Stephen M. Lacy
Vice President, Finance and Administration:
    Max Runciman

Meredith Corporation
Chairman and Chief Executive Officer: William T. Kerr

Chairman of the Executive Committee: E. T. Meredith III

All of us at Better Homes and Gardens® Books are dedicated to providing you with information and ideas to create beautiful and useful projects. We welcome your comments and suggestions. Write to us at: Better Homes and Gardens Books, Crafts Editorial Department, 1716 Locust Street—LN112, Des Moines, IA 50309-3023.

If you would like to purchase any of our books, check wherever quality books are sold. Visit us online at bhgbooks.com.

Cover: Photographer—Scott Little

Our seal assures you that every recipe in *Christmas: 101 Wondrous Ideas* has been tested in the Better Homes and Gardens® Test Kitchen. This means that each recipe is practical and reliable, and meets our high standards of taste appeal. We guarantee your satisfaction with this book for as long as you own it.

a Time of Wonder...

The Christmas season stirs up magic like no other time of year. It seems the closer we get to that special day each December, the more we open our arms and hearts to those we hold dear. Isn't it wonderful?

That's one reason we put so much love into celebrating the holiday. Many of us can go an entire year without doing much to change our surroundings, but as Christmas draws near, we turn into merry little elves transforming our homes into glistening wonderlands fit for Santa himself. (Not to mention filling the kitchen with holiday goodies!)

We also have an unending passion to show loved ones how much we care. For us creative types, nothing brings more happiness than surprising someone with a gift we have lovingly created especially for them. In turn, our hearts are overwhelmed with joy as we receive each thoughtful gesture of appreciation.

That's why we've created this inspiring book—because we equally treasure the Christmas spirit and want to share the warmth and wonder of it all.

So whether you find a new favorite recipe, a wintry decoration, or the perfect craft project to make for gift giving, our hope is that each page adds to the happiness of this coming Christmas and every one to come.

With merry holiday wishes to you and yours!

Carol Field Dahlstrom

contents

COME ALONG AS WE SHARE
DO-IT-YOURSELF IDEAS
THAT WILL PUT EVERYONE
IN THE HOLIDAY SPIRIT.
FROM WONDERFUL GIFT
IDEAS AND DELICIOUS
RECIPES TO TRIMS THAT
WILL TRANSFORM YOUR
HOME INTO A CHRISTMAS
WONDERLAND, YOU'LL
FIND ENDLESS INSPIRATION
IN EACH OF THESE
FESTIVE CHAPTERS.

CHAPTER 1

'Tis the Season

Warm the house in a
blanket of festivity
that puts everyone in
the holiday spirit.
From keepsake
stockings to last-minute
table and mantel
arrangements, you'll
create lasting
memories for friends
and family.

CHAPTER 2

Simple Gifts

Share your creativity
with those you love
this Christmas with
handmade treasures.
Whether you're looking
for projects to make or
wondrous new ways to
wrap your gifts, you'll
find dozens of great
ideas for gift giving in
this fun chapter.

4

CHAPTER 3

Sweetest Goodies

Treat your holiday guests to delectable homemade temptations, such as Chocolate Cherry Cookies, Fruited Truffles, and Pumpkin Swirl Cheesecake. You're sure to find new favorite recipes to become part of your holiday traditions.

CHAPTER 4

Trim the Tree

Deck the tree with glorious holiday ornaments the whole family will enjoy making. This inspiring chapter will show you how to use paint, beads, crafting foam, paper, and other materials to make grand Christmas tree decorations.

CHAPTER 5

Light the Way

Illuminate your holiday home, indoors and out, with these spectacular lighting ideas. Elegant candle displays, ice luminarias, and mesh icicles are a sampling of the bright projects you'll find to make your home glow with Christmas magic.

'Tis The

Season

a wonderland of white

A DEPARTURE FROM TRADITIONAL RED AND GREEN, THIS DISPLAY IS A BREATH OF FRESH WINTER AIR. ITEMS IN CREAMY SHADES OF WHITE ARE RICH WITH SHAPE AND TEXTURE. A FLUTED DISH CRADLES A PILLAR CANDLE DRIPPING WITH STRINGS OF PEARLS. A DELICATE GLASS BASKET HOLDS ALL-WHITE CANDY CANES, AND PURCHASED WHITE CHOCOLATES WAIT ON A PEDESTAL TO TEMPT ALL. ARRANGE THESE PRETTIES ON A SOFT FABRIC AND TUCK IN WHITE POINSETTIAS TO COMPLETE THE LOOK.

welcoming wreaths

Hang a wreath on the front door to put visitors in the holiday spirit before they enter. Choose the traditional or playful styles shown on these two pages or the sweet-as-can-be gumdrop wreath on page 12.

POINSETTIA WREATH

SUPPLIES

Wire cutters; ruler
1 large artificial purple poinsettia
7 medium artificial purple poinsettias
7 medium and 7 small artificial red poinsettias
24-inch green artificial wreath
7 stems of artificial blue grapes
14 assorted wired bulbs in red and purple
4 yards of 2½-inch-wide gold wired ribbon
Scissors

WHAT TO DO

1 Cut poinsettia stems to measure 8 to 10 inches. Arrange the poinsettias on the wreath. Poke the stems into the wreath and wind the wire stems around the wreath to secure.

2 Insert the grape stems around the wreath, spacing evenly. Wind the wire stems around the wreath. Add wired bulbs as desired.

3 Loosely wind the ribbon through the wreath, leaving loops. Trim the ribbon ends.

COOKIE CUTTER WREATH

SUPPLIES

Approximately 30 metal cookie cutters
Tacky wax
Small paper clips
3 yards of 1-inch-wide red-and-white check ribbon; scissors

WHAT TO DO

1 On a flat work surface, arrange the cookie cutters in a circle. Make sure all of the cutters have contact points.

2 Secure the contact points

CONTINUED ON PAGE 13

with tacky wax and small paper clips. This temporary adhesion will allow you to disassemble the wreath and keep your cutters for cookie making. Turn the wreath shape over.

3 Tie a ribbon bow. Paper-clip it to the wreath top. Trim the ribbon ends

GUMDROP WREATH

SUPPLIES
12-inch foam, such as Styrofoam, flat wreath form
Green spearmint candy leaves in a variety of shapes and sizes
Straight pins
Sharp knife
Cutting board
Small red gumdrops
1-inch-wide light green ribbon
½-inch-wide dark green ribbon
Fine wire
Scissors

WHAT TO DO
1 Decide on the placement of the various spearmint leaves on the foam wreath. Begin pinning the leaves around the inner edge of the foam wreath, overlapping the leaves to hide the pins and the foam. If the leaves are too thick, cut them in half on a cutting board. Continue pinning leaves in place until the circle is complete.

2 Pin leaves around the outer edge of the wreath, again overlapping the leaves. Pin leaves between the outer and inner edges of leaves, turning as necessary to cover the foam shape.

3 Cut the bottoms off the red gumdrops to make them shorter. Push pins into the leaves where red gumdrops are desired, leaving about one-quarter of each pin exposed. Press the gumdrops onto the pin head.

4 Combine the ribbons to make a generous bow. Wire it to the top of the wreath. Trim the ribbon ends.

Note: This wreath is for decoration only. Be sure to hang out of reach of children.

center of attention

CREATE A BUZZ AROUND YOUR HOLIDAY TABLE WITH AN UNEXPECTED BOWL CENTERPIECE THAT WILL GET YOUR GUESTS TALKING.

SPARKLING SNOWBALLS

SUPPLIES

White wax or paraffin for candle making; hammer
Metal can, larger than foam balls
Old pan
Hot plate or stove
2- to 4-inch-diameter plastic foam balls, such as Styrofoam
Toothpick
Pan of cold water larger than foam balls
White glitter
Waxed paper

WHAT TO DO

1 Break up wax with a hammer. Place it in the can. Put water in an old pan and place on a hot plate or stove. Place the can in the water and bring water to a simmer, melting wax slowly. (Note: Never melt wax in a microwave or directly on the stove. Also, never leave melting wax unattended.)

2 After the wax has melted, turn off the heat. Put a toothpick in a foam ball. Dip the ball into the wax and then into the cold water. Repeat until the ball resembles a snowball. After the last dip in hot wax, sprinkle glitter over the shape. Lay on waxed paper to dry.

3 Arrange the snowballs in a bowl of flocked greenery with other trims as desired.

3 *For the framed photos,* disassemble the frames. Apply gold leaf to the frames as for the candles, *below left.* Place photos in the frames and reassemble.

4 *To arrange the centerpiece,* tuck the balls and framed photos in the bowl, but let them spill out onto the table as well. Embellish with roses, tinsel, and greenery. Place candles around the centerpiece. For a fun surprise, put special framed photos facedown beside each place setting and leave them that way until the meal is over. Then have everyone turn their photos over and share their memories.

Note: Never leave burning candles unattended.

GILDED MEMORIES

SUPPLIES
Tissue paper
Christmas balls
Decoupage medium
Paintbrush
Gold spray paint
Gold-leaf fixative
  (available at
  crafts stores)
Old or new candles
Gold leaf
Framed photos

Clear glass bowl
Tinsel
Greenery
Roses

WHAT TO DO

1 *For the Christmas balls,* tear pieces of tissue paper and crumple them. Paint decoupage medium on an ornament where tissue paper is desired. Press the crumpled paper on the decoupage medium and let dry. In a well-ventilated work area, spray-paint the ornaments gold. Let dry.

2 *For the candles,* spray on gold-leaf fixative. Lay gold-leaf sheets on top of the fixative. Peel the sheets back, leaving the gold leaf in the sprayed areas.

HERE ARE WINTRY DECORATIONS THE WHOLE FAMILY WILL ENJOY MAKING. AMONG THE MIX YOU'LL FIND PRETTY ORIGAMI TRIMS AND EMBOSSED SNOWFLAKES TO START THE FUN.

DECORATIVE TREE

SUPPLIES

Saw
Tree branch
White spray paint
8-inch-square papier-mâché box
Art paper in 2 or more shades
Tape; ruler; pencil
Scissors; glue stick
Floral foam

WHAT TO DO

1 Cut a branch to the desired height. In a well-ventilated work area, spray-paint the branch white. Let dry. For the base, wrap the box with art paper. Cut diamonds 6 inches tall and 3 inches wide. Glue the diamonds to the box as shown in the photo, *opposite,* wrapping the excess length over the top and bottom edges. Fill the box with florist's foam and insert the branch.

EMBOSSED SNOWFLAKES

SUPPLIES

Snowflake stamp, approximately 2¾ inches
Silver, opaque pigment stamp pad
White art paper
Crystal embossing powder; heat gun
Scissors

WHAT TO DO

1 Press the stamp onto a silver stamp pad and then onto white art paper. Sprinkle with crystal embossing powder, and use a heat gun on the image until the powder melts. Cut out around the snowflake, leaving a thin paper border.

PINECONE GARLAND

SUPPLIES

Small pinecones
Spray paint in white and blue
Drill and fine bit
Fine wire

WHAT TO DO

1 Spray-paint small pinecones white, followed with a mist of blue paint. Drill small holes through pinecones and string on thin wire.

SNOWFLAKE TABLECLOTH AND NAPKINS

SUPPLIES

Tracing paper
Sharp pencil
Purchased paper tablecloths in cream and blue
Small sharp scissors, such as scherenschnitte or cuticle
Purchased paper napkins in cream and blue

WHAT TO DO

1 *For the tablecloth,* trace the snowflake pattern, *page 18,* onto tracing paper. Use a copy machine to copy a variety of larger and smaller snowflakes. Randomly position the snowflake copies underneath the cream tablecloth; use pencil to lightly trace snowflakes onto tablecloth. Use scissors to cut out snowflakes. Place blue tablecloth on table. Layer the cream tablecloth over the blue tablecloth.

CONTINUED ON PAGE 18

2 *For napkins,* trace, cut, and layer as for the tablecloth, cutting through the top layer of the folded napkin. Alternate colors if desired, cutting snowflakes from blue to layer over cream.

ORIGAMI STARS

SUPPLIES
Assorted art paper in 5½- and 3⅞-inch squares
Fine wire

WHAT TO DO
1 Firmly crease each fold to make a flexible crease. Refer to the origami diagrams, *opposite,* when folding.

2 Layer the two sizes of paper (Diagram 1); treat as one. Fold paper in half vertically; unfold. Fold in half horizontally; unfold. Fold from top left corner to bottom right corner; unfold. Fold from top right corner to bottom left corner; unfold.

3 Fold the corners to meet in the center (Diagram 2). Fold the square in half to make a triangle, bringing bottom corner up to meet top corner (Diagram 3).

4 Hold the top points of the triangle together and bring the bottom points up to meet the top point, letting sides of the triangle open. Tuck the points between the front and back layers (Diagram 4). Flatten paper into a small square with two layers.

5 Fold each side corner of the front layer to the center crease line (Diagram 5); unfold. Fold the bottom point up to the center crease line (Diagram 6); unfold. For flexible creases, work folds back and forth. Turn the square over and repeat steps for Diagrams 5 and 6.

TABLECLOTH AND NAPKIN SNOWFLAKE PATTERN

6 Working with the top layer of the square, pull down the top corner as shown in Diagram 7. Fold along creases made in Diagram steps 5 and 6, creating the shape shown in Diagram 8. Turn figure over and repeat Diagram steps 7 and 8 with remaining layer of square, creating the diamond shape shown in Diagram 9.

7 Bring bottom point of diamond up to meet top point (Diagram 10).

Turn figure over and repeat Diagram step 10, creating the shape shown in Diagram 11.

8 Referring to Diagram 12, pull out the two points that are sandwiched between the top and bottom layers, creating the finished snowflake shown in Diagram 13.

9 For the hanger, make a fishhook shape with fine wire. Poke the straight end of the wire through one point of the snowflake. Fold the end up and twist.

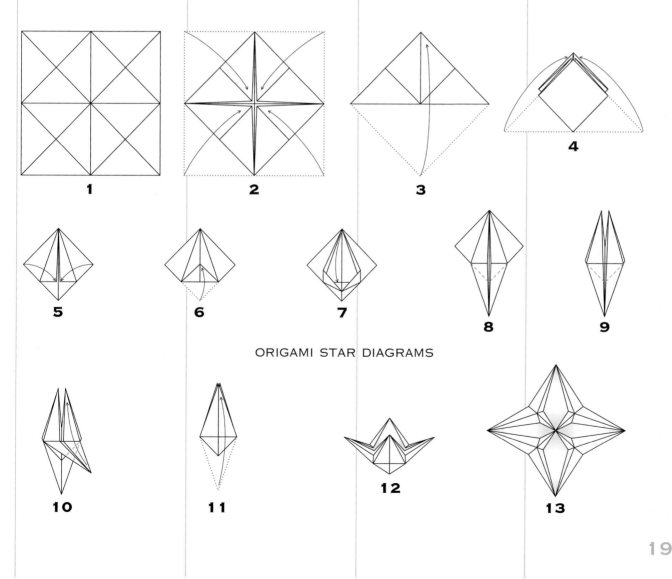

ORIGAMI STAR DIAGRAMS

merry mantels

Drape your mantel with a contemporary version of a popcorn garland or let nature take center stage with the mantel trims, opposite. Instructions for all trims start on page 22.

GARLAND
OF GOODIES

GARLAND OF GOODIES

SUPPLIES

Small star-shape Vanilla Cutouts cookies (recipe, *right*)
Royal icing
Food coloring
Edible glitter
Fresh cranberries
Popcorn
Thin (about 28-gauge) silver wire
½-inch-wide satin ribbon, cut into 12-inch lengths

WHAT TO DO

1 Bake cookies as directed in Vanilla Cutouts recipe, *right*. Tint royal icing in desired colors with food coloring. Frost cooled cookies. While frosting is wet, sprinkle with edible glitter. Let dry.

2 Alternately string cranberries and popcorn onto wire. Allow a little slack at each end to make loops for hanging. String a length of ribbon through the hole in the top of each cookie. At desired intervals, slide the cranberry and popcorn apart slightly and tie the ribbon around the wire, letting the cookie hang from the garland.

VANILLA CUTOUTS

SUPPLIES

4 cups all-purpose flour
1 teaspoon baking powder
½ teaspoon salt
1 cup butter (no substitutes)
1 cup sugar
⅔ cup light corn syrup
1 tablespoon vanilla
1 egg, beaten
Star cookie cutters
Cookie sheet

WHAT TO DO

1 Stir together flour, baking powder, and salt; set aside.

2 Combine butter, sugar, and corn syrup in a small saucepan. Cook and stir over medium heat until butter is melted and sugar is dissolved. Pour into a large bowl. Stir in vanilla. Cool for 5 minutes. Add egg; mix well.

3 Add flour mixture to egg mixture; stir until combined. Divide dough in half. Cover and chill at least 2 hours. (If the dough chills overnight, let it stand 5 to 10 minutes at room temperature before rolling.)

4 Roll each portion on a lightly floured surface until ⅛ inch thick. Cut into desired shapes with floured cookie cutters or a sharp knife. Place cutouts 1 inch apart on an ungreased cookie sheet. Poke a hole at the top of each cookie using a drinking straw.

5 Bake in a 375° oven for 8 to 10 minutes or until edges are lightly browned. Cool on cookie sheet for 1 minute. Transfer cookies to wire rack and cool completely. Makes 24.

NATURE'S PRESENTATION

SUPPLIES
Greenery
Twigs
Gilded seedpods
Scissors
Pillar candles
Floral tape or a
  rubber band
Raffia or ribbon
Straight pins

WHAT TO DO

1 Decide which natural materials will be used to decorate each candle. Cut the lengths of the greenery, twigs, or seedpods, if necessary, to be shorter than the candle.

2 Use floral tape or a rubber band to hold the natural items in place around the base of the candle.

3 Tie raffia or ribbon over the floral tape or rubber band. Trim the ribbon ends if desired.

4 For the pod-covered candle, pin the pods in a pattern or randomly on the candle.

Note: Never leave burning candles unattended.

PINECONE PARADE

SUPPLIES
Newspapers
Pinecones
White acrylic paint
Paintbrush
White glitter, optional
Short colored bottles
  without stoppers
Hot-glue gun and
  glue sticks
Colored raffia
Scissors

WHAT TO DO

1 Cover the work surface with newspapers. Paint the edges of the pinecones to give a snowy appearance. If desired, sprinkle the wet paint with glitter. Let dry.

2 Wash and dry the bottles. Place a pinecone on the top of each bottle. Add a drop of hotmelt adhesive to secure.

3 Tie several strands of raffia around the neck of the bottle. Tie the ends into a bow. Trim the raffia ends as desired.

fruit pyramid

WITH A BASE
MADE OF STACKED
SILVERY BUCKETS,
THIS STUNNING
FRUIT
CENTERPIECE
TAKES JUST
MINUTES
TO MAKE.

SUPPLIES

Galvanized buckets
 in graduated sizes
Floral foam
3 kinds of fruit in
 graduated sizes,
 such as pears,
 lemons, and apples
Wood florist's picks
1 pineapple
Boxwood clippings,
 myrtle sprigs, or
 other fresh
 greenery

WHAT TO DO

1 Pack each bucket
full of floral foam.
Stack the buckets,
aligning the handles.

2 Secure the fruit
to the foam with
florist's picks. Arrange
so all fruit points in
the same direction.
Use two florist's picks
to secure a pineapple
to the top.

3 Tuck greenery
between each
piece of fruit to hide
the foam and to drape
over the edges of
the buckets.

INTRICATE APPLIQUÉ, EMBROIDERY, AND BEADING EMBELLISH THIS SCANDINAVIAN STOCKING.

SUPPLIES

Tracing paper
Pencil
Scissors
½ yard of green wool fabric
½ yard of lining fabric
Fusible transweb paper
9½×19-inch and 5×1-inch pieces of red wool fabric
6×6-inch piece of light green wool fabric
6×6-inch piece of gold wool fabric

CONTINUED ON PAGE 26

winter wool stocking

3×3-inch piece of bright green wool fabric

Matching rayon thread for machine embroidery; needle

Embroidery floss in black and gold

16 small red faceted beads; 3 small black faceted beads

9 sew-on gold rhinestones

2 yards of black sew-in piping

1 yard of ½-inch-wide black trim

WHAT TO DO

1 Enlarge and trace the stocking pattern, *right.* Cut out the stocking front and back from green wool and from lining fabric.

2 Trace the full-size shapes, *opposite,* onto transweb paper and fuse to the corresponding wool fabrics. Cut out.

3 Fuse the shapes to the front, following the product directions. Machine-appliqué with matching threads around the leaves and five large red flowers.

4 Using black floss, add stem stitches, *opposite.* Add gold straight stitches and French knots on the two center flowers. Sew on the beads and rhinestones.

5 Stitch piping along outside edge except at the top. Stitch stocking front to back. Trim and clip seam; turn.

6 Press the hanger piece in half lengthwise. Bring the raw edges to the fold; stitch to secure. Referring to the photo on *page 25,* tack the black trim on the red cuff. Sew the cuff piece together at the short ends; press open. Press cuff in half lengthwise with wrong sides together.

7 Place the cuff over the stocking top with raw edges together. Stitch the cuff to the stocking.

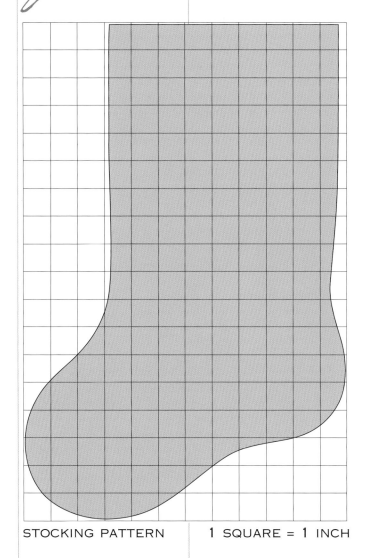

STOCKING PATTERN   **1 SQUARE = 1 INCH**

8 Stitch lining pieces together, leaving an opening for turning. Slip stocking into lining. With hanger in place, stitch around top edge. Pull the stocking through the lining opening. Stitch the opening closed. Fold the cuff up and stitch around the stocking top and lining. Fold the cuff over. Press if desired.

WINTER WOOL STOCKING
APPLIQUÉ PATTERNS

FRENCH KNOT

STEM STITCH

STRAIGHT STITCH

AS QUAINT AS
GRANDMA'S
PIECED QUILTS,
THESE STOCKINGS
LEND
OLD-FASHIONED
CHARM TO THE
HOLIDAY MANTEL.

JACOB'S LADDER
STOCKING

SUPPLIES

For each stocking:
Tracing paper
Pencil; scissors
Tape measure; three
   9½-inch completed
   quilt blocks
1 fat quarter of plaid
   for stocking back
½ yard of
   coordinating fabric
   for lining and cuff
12×18-inch piece of
   coordinating fabric
   for piping
1⅓ yards of small
   piping cord
Fleece; interfacing
Needle; thread
Buttons, ribbon, bell,
   and cording

WHAT TO DO

1 Enlarge and trace
the patterns,
pages 30–31. From
coordinating fabric cut:
- 2 stocking patterns;
   1 in reverse for
   lining
- One 10½×17¾-inch
   strip for cuff
- One 1¼×6-inch
   strip for loop

stockings

From second coordinating fabric, cut:

- Enough 1½-inch-wide bias strips to total 46 inches in length for piping

From fleece, cut:

- 2 stocking patterns

2 To prepare the Jacob's Ladder blocks, *page 31*, make AA unit (6 times). Make BBB unit (9 times); combine three BBB units to make nine-patch (3 times). Sew two AA units with B unit on one end (2 times) for top and bottom strips. Sew two AA units with B unit in the center for center strip. Sew top and bottom strips to center strip.

3 To prepare the Country Pinwheel blocks, *page 30*, use the pattern or cut 3⅛-inch squares in half diagonally to equal two A triangles. Cut a total of 16 dark A triangles and 16 light A triangles. Sew one light A and one dark A together along long edges. Make a total of 16 AA units. Join the AA units together into two rows; then add the next two rows to make a block.

4 Sew two blocks together vertically. Add a third block to the left side of the bottom block, horizontally as shown in Diagrams on *pages 30–31*. Only a small portion of third block will be used.

5 Lay fleece onto the wrong side of the front and back stocking. Baste and quilt as desired.

6 Piece the 1½-inch bias strips to total 46 inches in length. Cover the piping cord with the bias strip. Position the piping on the right side of the stocking front, at the seam line with the raw edges together. Stitch the piping to the stocking, beginning at the top side edge and continuing to the other top side edge of the stocking. Trim the piping to match the stocking edge.

7 With the right sides together, sew the front to the back. Clip the seams and press. Turn stocking right side out.

8 Stabilize the cuff with interfacing. Sew the 10½×17¾-inch strip together at the short ends. This will form the back seam of the cuff. Press the seam open. Press the cuff in half lengthwise with the wrong sides together.

9 Position the cuff over the top of the stocking

with the raw edges together. Position the seam at the back of the stocking. Fold the piping toward the front as you stitch the cuff to the stocking.

10 Press a ¼-inch hem lengthwise on each side of the 1¼×6-inch strip for a loop. Fold in half lengthwise, press, and topstitch

CONTINUED ON PAGE 30

COUNTRY PINWHEEL STOCKING

along the edge. Fold the loop in half. Baste the raw edges together at the top of the cuff behind the piping at the stocking back side seam.

11 With the right sides together, sew the lining front to the lining back, leaving an opening in one side seam for turning. Clip; press the seams open.

12 Slip stocking into the lining, right sides together, matching seams. Sew around the top edge and trim. Turn to right side by pulling the stocking through lining side seam opening. Stitch opening closed. Press lining to the inside of stocking. Turn cuff down over top of the stocking. Press.

13 Add trims as desired.

COUNTRY PINWHEEL STOCKING ASSEMBLY DIAGRAM

COUNTRY
PINWHEEL
TRIANGLE
PATTERN

COUNTRY PINWHEEL
STOCKING DIAGRAM

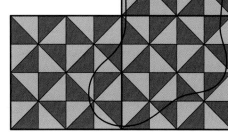

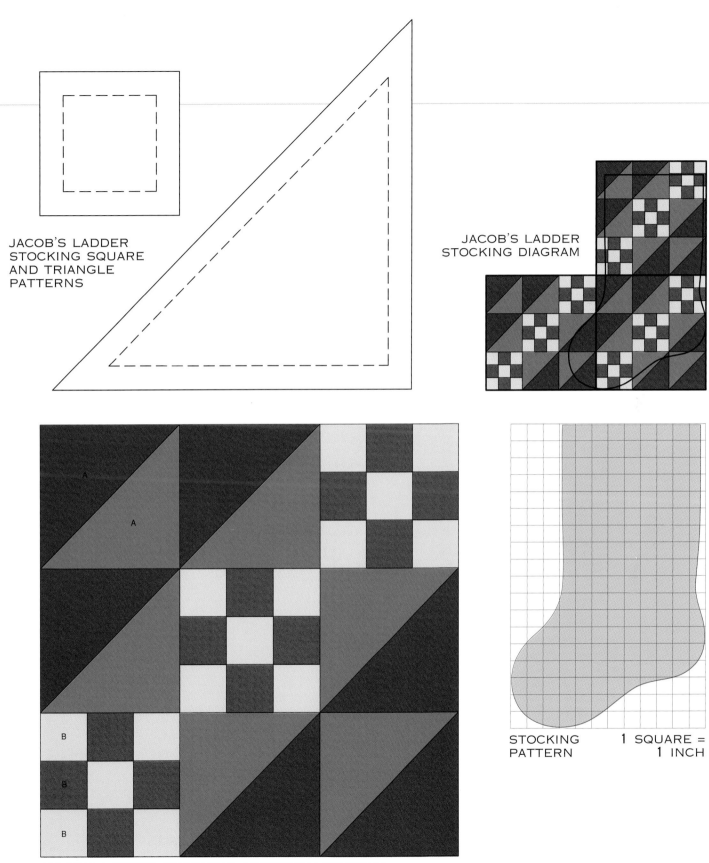

JACOB'S LADDER
STOCKING SQUARE
AND TRIANGLE
PATTERNS

JACOB'S LADDER
STOCKING DIAGRAM

JACOB'S LADDER STOCKING ASSEMBLY DIAGRAM

STOCKING
PATTERN

1 SQUARE =
1 INCH

31

snowfall flowerpots

THE KIDS WILL BE PROUD WHEN YOU USE THEIR PAPER SNOWFLAKES TO MAKE THESE LOVELY HOLIDAY FLOWERPOTS. THE SNOWFLAKES ACT AS STENCILS FOR THE SPARKLY METALLIC BLUE SPRAY PAINT.

SUPPLIES
Paper
Scissors; iron
Newspapers
Terra-cotta flowerpots
Spray paint in white
  and metallic blue
Temporary spray
  adhesive
Pinecones
Greenery to plant

WHAT TO DO
1 Cut out paper snowflakes in various sizes. Iron flat.

2 In a well-ventilated work area, cover the work surface with newspapers. Spray-paint the flowerpots white. Let dry. Spray the back of the paper snowflakes with temporary adhesive. Place the snowflakes randomly on painted flowerpots. Spray-paint the pots metallic blue. Let the paint dry and remove the paper snowflakes.

3 Spray-paint the pinecones blue. Let dry.

4 Plant desired greenery in the flowerpots. Place pinecones on top of the soil.

SUPPLIES

**¼-inch-diameter
  dowels; yardstick
Saw; green floral wire
Evergreen cuttings
Kumquats
Blueberries
Raspberries
Miniature squash
Hot-glue gun and
  glue sticks**

WHAT TO DO

1 Cut 32- and 24-inch lengths of dowel for the cross. For the vertical angled pieces, cut four 18-inch lengths. For the horizontal angled pieces, cut four 15-inch lengths. Arrange the dowels as shown, *below.* Secure the intersections with wire.

2 Cover the form with evergreen cuttings, attaching pieces with floral wire.

3 Use hot glue to attach assorted fruits as desired in a border around the swag. Also use hot glue to fill in with more evergreens, if needed.

Note: The berries in this swag will last a few days outside in cold weather. Citrus fruits and squash will last longer. Use artificial fruits and berries for a longer-lasting wreath.

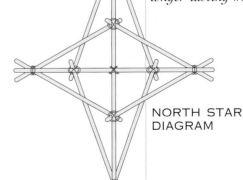

NORTH STAR
DIAGRAM

BRIGHTEN YOUR ENTRYWAY WITH EVERGREEN CUTTINGS ACCENTED WITH KUMQUATS, BLUEBERRIES, RASPBERRIES, AND MINIATURE SQUASH.

TREAT YOUR BACKYARD BIRDS WITH THESE ONE-OF-A-KIND ICE RINGS FILLED WITH SCRUMPTIOUS DELIGHTS. HANG THE RINGS NEARBY SO YOU CAN ENJOY WATCHING YOUR FEATHERED FRIENDS.

glistening ice rings

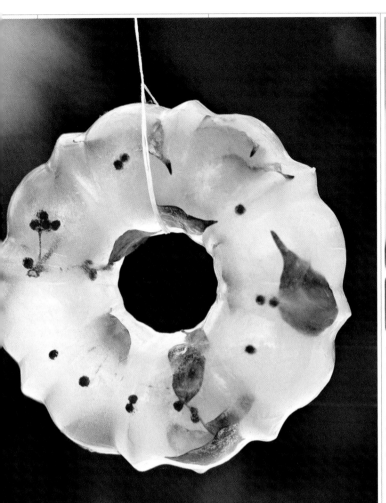

ICE RING
PREPARATION

SUPPLIES

**Gelatin ring molds
or mini aluminum
pie tins**
**Plastic disposable
cups**
Water
Cranberries
Birdseed; sticks
String

WHAT TO DO

1 Use a ring mold
or place a plastic
cup in the center of
the pie tin. If using a
cup, put some water
in it so it does not
float in the pie tin.
Fill the mold or the
pie tin halfway with
water as shown in the
photo, *above*.

2 Arrange the
cranberries,
sticks, and birdseed in
the water. Let the ring
freeze until solid.

3 To remove the
ring from the
mold, run cold water
over the back of the
ring. Remove the cup.
Tie or loop string
around the ring and
hang in a tree or bush.

popcorn stars

DURING THE COLD WEATHER, FEATHERED AND FURRY VISITORS WILL APPRECIATE GOOD-TO-EAT POPCORN TREATS.

SUPPLIES
Wire cutters
Needle-nose pliers
18-gauge aluminum wire
Ruler
Popped popcorn

WHAT TO DO

1 Using pliers, twist two 12-inch pieces and one 16-inch piece of wire together at their centers to form a star shape. Slide popcorn onto each spoke, leaving space on end of long wire.

2 Loop ends of spokes to keep popcorn in place. Hang on tree using a looped end of the long wire.

SUPPLIES

Wire cutters
Floral wire; ruler
Fresh or artificial
  greenery
Gold artificial fruit
  on wires, stems, or
  in clusters
Gold lotus pads
Miniature gifts
  wrapped in gold
  paper
Gold snowflake
  ornaments
White Christmas
  lights
Beaded garland
4 yards of 3-inch-wide
  dark green velvet
  ribbon
2 yards of
  1½-inch-wide
  green-and-red
  plaid ribbon
Scissors

WHAT TO DO

1 Cut several pieces
  of wire, each
6 to 10 inches long.
Use wires to connect
greenery into a garland
of desired length.

2 Arrange fruit,
  lotus pads,
miniature gifts,
snowflakes, or other
embellishments on the
garland. Wire the
items in place.

3 Wind Christmas
  lights through
the garland, securing
loosely with wire
pieces. Wire the
garland to a railing or
other structure.

4 Arrange beaded
  garland to
drape in large scallops
from the bottom of the
greenery. Use wires to
secure the beads.

5 Tie a large bow
  using the velvet
ribbon. Tie a small
bow with the plaid
ribbon. Combine the
bows and wire to one
end of the garland.

DISPLAY THIS
GILDED NATURE
GARLAND ON YOUR
PORCH RAILING, IN
A WINDOW BOX, OR
ALONG THE FENCE.

ELEGANTLY
DRAPED WITH
STRINGS OF GOLD
BEADS, IT WILL BE
THE TALK OF YOUR
NEIGHBORHOOD.

garland of gold

mosaic ornaments

MOSAIC ORNAMENTS ADD CHRISTMAS COLOR TO A WINTER LANDSCAPE. BROKEN TILE PIECES COVER BIG PLASTIC FOAM BALLS, CREATING A MOUND OF GLORIOUS HUES. STACK THE COLORFUL BALLS OR HANG THEM FROM TREES. LEAVE THEM OUT AFTER THE SNOW MELTS FOR LOVELY SUMMER GARDEN ACCESSORIES.

SUPPLIES

Ceramic tiles in assorted colors (inexpensive scraps or extras)
Clear plastic bag or drop cloth
Hammer; yardstick
Aluminum wire
Wire cutters; stick
Plastic foam balls
Buckets or chairs
Mastic; butter knife
Sponge; grout
Exterior grout sealer

WHAT TO DO

1 Place tiles inside clear plastic bag or drop cloth; hit with hammer to break into small pieces.

2 Cut a piece of wire about 22 inches long. Poke through center of plastic foam ball so end comes out the opposite side. Bend the wire end back toward the ball, push it up into the ball so it is flush against the ball and secure. For easier working, wind the remaining end of wire around a stick. Place stick on two buckets or two chairs so that ball is hanging, as shown, *above.*

3 Use butter knife to cover plastic foam ball with mastic. Press broken tile into mastic, covering the ball as desired. Let mastic dry according to manufacturer's instructions.

4 Mix and use grout according to manufacturer's instructions. Spread it over entire ball, making sure to fill all the spaces between the tiles. Scrape most of excess off tiles. When grout has set, use a damp (not wet) sponge to wipe remaining grout from tiles.

5 When grout is completely dry, spray with exterior grout sealer and let dry. Hang balls from trees using wire as a hanger or cut off wire as close to ball as possible and stack in a birdbath.

smiling snowmen

SNOWMEN ARE ALWAYS A MERRY SYMBOL OF THE SEASON AND THESE SNOW FRIENDS ARE NO EXCEPTION. USE THIS TRIO FOR INSPIRATION. THEN HAVE FUN CREATING YOUR OWN HAPPY EXPRESSIONS AND WINTER WEAR.

SUPPLIES

Various sizes of foam balls, such as Styrofoam
Toothpick
Thick white crafts glue
Acini di pepe pasta
Bowl
Paintbrush
Spoon
Twigs
White acrylic paint
Doll hats or old socks; scissors
⅛-inch-wide ribbon
Fabric stiffener
Orange polymer clay, such as Sculpey
Baking dish
Hot-glue gun and glue sticks
Black fabric paint
Buttons; pom-poms
1-inch-wide ribbon

WHAT TO DO

1 Press the foam ball for the snowman body against a hard, flat surface so the snowman will stand up. Coat one end of the toothpick with glue and push it into the top of the foam ball. Coat the exposed toothpick end with glue and push a second foam ball on top of the toothpick as shown in Photo 1, *right*. Let dry.

2 Pour acini di pepe in a bowl. Paint crafts glue over one side of the foam balls. Spoon acini di pepe over the wet glue as shown in Photo 2. Continue until all but the bottom is covered. Push the twig arms into place, securing with glue. Let dry.

3 Paint the snowman white. Let dry.

4 To make a hat from a sock, cut the cuff off. Tie a ribbon bow around the cut-off end as shown in Photo 3. Dip in fabric stiffener and place on the snowman's head. Let dry.

5 From orange clay, make a carrot-shape nose as shown in Photo 3. Bake on a baking dish as directed by the clay manufacturer's instructions. Let cool. Hot-glue the nose to the snowman's face. Let dry.

6 Draw on two round eyes and a smile using black fabric paint. Let dry.

7 Glue buttons, pom-pom earmuffs, ribbon scarves, and purchased hats in place. Let dry.

Simple

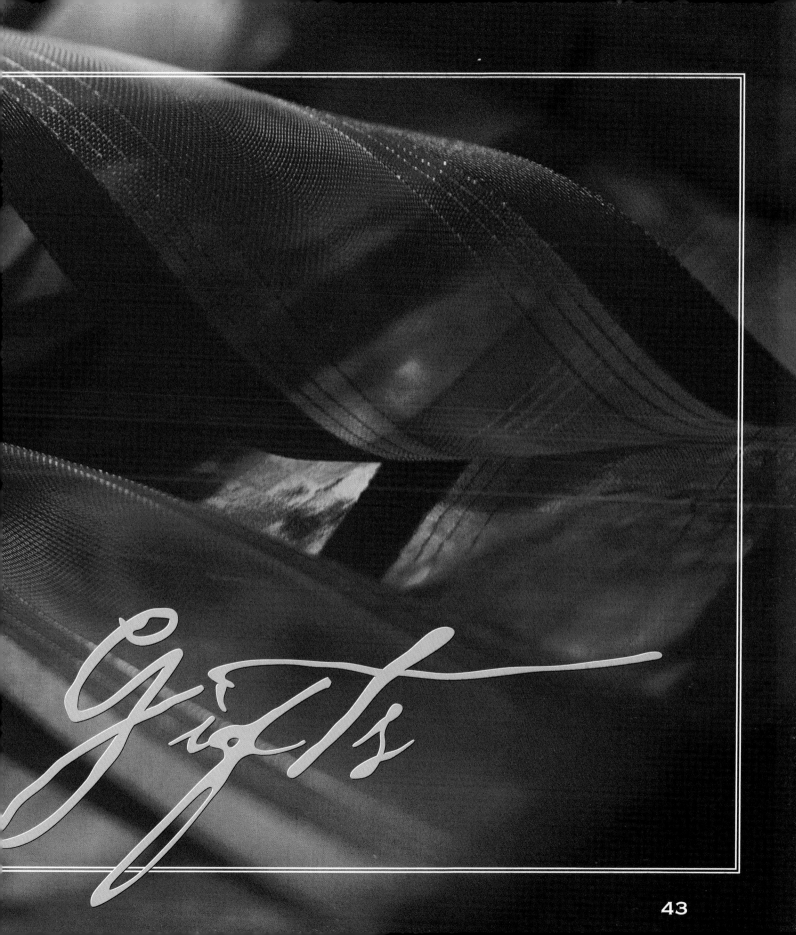

Gifts

vintage pin trims

Gather holiday pins from your Grandmother's or Mother's jewelry box and you'll have the sparkle you need for simple gift trims. Start by purchasing solid-colored gift bags. Tie bows from coordinating ribbons. Pin the vintage jewelry piece on or near the center of the bow. If desired, hang a gift tag from the pin.

woven ribbon bag

JUST THE RIGHT SIZE FOR HOLDING A SMALL SURPRISE, THIS BAG IS WOVEN FROM SCRAPS OF HOLIDAY RIBBONS. A PRETTY RED AND GREEN BUTTON ADDS THE FINISHING TOUCH.

SUPPLIES

Scissors; ¼ yard of lightweight fusible interfacing; pins
Corrugated cardboard or foam-core board
Approximately 9 yards of ¼- to 1½-inch-wide ribbon
Fusible hem tape; iron
7×9-inch piece of lining fabric
Ruler
Thread to match ribbons
Needle
Snap and button
Purchased tassel

WHAT TO DO

1 Cut a 6½×22½-inch piece of interfacing. Pin the interfacing, fusible side up, to the cardboard.

2 Cut enough 22½-inch-long ribbons to cover the interfacing. Pin the ribbons side by side atop the interfacing.

3 Cut several ribbons to a length of 6½ inches. Pin fusible hem tape to the ribbon backs.

4 Begin weaving short ribbons with those pinned to the cardboard.

5 Pin the ribbon ends as the weaving is completed.

6 Using an iron, fuse the ribbons to the interfacing, removing the pins as you go. Trim the edges if necessary.

7 Place the lining fabric atop the woven ribbon piece, right sides facing. Stitch together using a ¼-inch seam allowance and leaving one short end open. Trim seams and turn.

8 Measure 4½ inches from stitched short end. Fold the woven piece at this point with right sides facing. Hand-stitch both side seams. Turn right side out.

9 To make the flap point, measure 2½ inches from open end on each side. Fold the corners together and stitch from marked sides to center of flap. Turn right side out.

10 Sew on a snap closure where flap point meets the bag. Sew a button and tassel to the point of the flap.

May this Christmas Season and the New Year bring you Peace and Happiness.

FRAME YOUR FAVORITE SEASONAL SENTIMENTS WITH SWEET-SMELLING SCENTS. THESE SMALL HOLIDAY DECORATIONS MAKE GREAT GIFTS AND ARE A GOOD RECYCLING PROJECT FOR THE KIDS.

SUPPLIES
Pencil; ruler
Recycled Christmas
 card with saying
Scissors
Red marking pen
Paper in red and
 green
Glue stick
Cinnamon sticks
Hot-glue gun and
 glue sticks
Gold cord

Gold-edge green ribbon

WHAT TO DO

1 Using a pencil and ruler, draw a box around the saying, leaving a border of approximately ½ inch. Cut out on the line. Outline the paper with red marking pen.

2 Cut a piece of green paper ¼ inch larger than the saying. Cut a piece of red paper 1 inch larger than the green paper. Glue the green paper on the red paper using a glue stick. Glue the saying on the green paper.

3 Choose eight cinnamon sticks that are longer than the paper rectangle. Hot-glue the cinnamon frame together with two sticks on the top, two on the bottom, and two on each side.

4 Tie a cord from the top corners for hanging. Wrap the intersecting corners with ribbon. Knot and trim ends as desired.

5 Hot-glue the frame to the mounted paper saying.

cinnamon stick wishes

pretty etched plates

ETCH A CLEAR OR COLORED GLASS PLATE WITH THE WORDS FROM A CHRISTMAS CAROL OR OTHER HOLIDAY GREETING. MOUND COOKIES OR CANDY ON THE DECORATIVE PLATE TO GIVE TO A HOSTESS.

SUPPLIES

Glass cleaner made to work with acid (sold alongside etching cream)
Glass plate or platter
Tape
Clear self-adhesive shelf covering
Fine-tip permanent marking pen
Crafts knife
Burnisher or an old credit card
Lint-free cloth
Newspapers
Foam paintbrush
Etching cream

WHAT TO DO

1 In a well-ventilated work area, clean the glass plate with the specified glass cleaner. (It is important to use the special glass cleaner because it won't leave a film.)

2 Create words on a computer, and use the printout for your pattern. Tape the pattern to the back of the plate.

3 Cover the plate front with clear self-adhesive shelf covering, piecing strips as needed to cover the surface completely. Trace the words with the permanent marking pen as shown in Photo 1, *right*. Remove the pattern from the back of the plate.

4 Cut out the letters using the crafts knife as shown in Photo 2. Press the edges of the letters firmly, using the burnisher or an old credit card to seal the edges. (Do not use your fingers. The oil from your skin may interfere with the action of the etching cream.)

5 To prepare the plate for etching, lightly reclean the exposed glass with the special glass cleaner. Use a damp (not wet) cloth. Pat dry.

6 Cover the work surface with newspapers before you begin working with the etching cream. Using the foam paintbrush, apply a thick layer of etching cream over the stencil cutouts as shown in Photo 3. Gently move the cream around the area to eliminate air bubbles. Wait 5 to 6 minutes. Rinse off the etching cream.

7 Remove shelf covering to expose etching. Wash plate thoroughly.

holiday treat jar

THIS BRIGHT CHRISTMAS TREE JAR IS PERFECT FOR THE SEASON'S SWEET SURPRISES.

SUPPLIES

Glass jar with lid
Newspapers
Disposable foam plate
Acrylic glass paints in green, white, purple, dark green, metallic gold, red, and yellow
Paintbrushes
Toothpick
Old toothbrush

WHAT TO DO

1 Before beginning to paint, wash the glassware and let it dry. Avoid touching the areas to be painted.

2 Cover your work surface with newspapers. On the plate, mix a small amount of green with white. Start to paint the snow at the bottom of the jar. Using the same colors, paint a large tree on each side of the jar. Mix a small amount of purple with white and continue painting the top of the snow. Let the paint dry.

3 Using dark green, paint small trees around the jar between the large trees. Add stars to the top of each large tree using metallic gold. Paint various sizes of gold stars on the lid. Let the paint dry.

4 To add trims to the large trees, dip the handle of a paintbrush into the desired colors of paint and dot on trees. For garlands, use a toothpick and metallic gold paint. Make several dots in a row. Let the paint dry.

5 Dip the bristles of an old toothbrush into white paint. Run your finger along the bristles to splatter specks of paint over the jar to resemble snow. Let the paint dry.

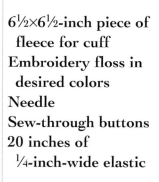

NO ONE WILL MIND BUNDLING UP FOR THE COLD WITH THESE DELIGHTFUL MITTENS THAT KEEP HANDS WARM.

SUPPLIES

FOR THE DENIM MITTENS

Tracing paper; pencil
Fusible web paper
Scissors; ruler
½ yard of denim fabric or pieces of jeans; ½ yard of lining fabric

6½×6½-inch piece of fleece for cuff
Embroidery floss in desired colors
Needle
Sew-through buttons
20 inches of ¼-inch-wide elastic

WHAT TO DO

1 Make two three-piece patchworks from denim, allowing enough fabric for mitten fronts.

2 Trim as desired using floss and stitches such as lazy daisy, feather, French knot, blanket, and straight stitches, *page 53*. Add buttons where desired.

3 Assemble the mittens as described, *page 52*.

SUPPLIES

FOR THE HEART AND STAR MITTENS

Tracing paper; pencil
Fusible web paper
Scissors; ruler
Needle

½ yard of print corduroy for mitten fabric
½ yard of lining fabric
6½×6½-inch piece of fleece for cuff
4×4-inch piece of imitation cloth suede, such as Ultrasuede, for each heart or star
1½×1½-inch pieces of imitation cloth suede in six colors for circles

CONTINUED ON PAGE 52

merry mittens

Embroidery floss in desired colors
20 inches of ¼-inch-wide elastic

WHAT TO DO

1 Trace patterns for heart or star and six circles, *page 55,* onto fusible web paper. Fuse to corresponding imitation suede. Cut out. Fuse to mitten front. Blanket-stitch around outside edge, *opposite,* using three plies of floss. Make a contrasting cuff from fleece with blanket stitches around the bottom edge.

2 Assemble the mittens as described *below.*

MITTEN ASSEMBLY

1 Enlarge and trace the mitten patterns, *right,* onto tracing paper and cut out. Cut shapes from mitten and lining fabrics (reversing the shapes for opposite mitten).

2 Stitch mitten seams with right sides facing using a ¼-inch seam allowance. Stitch the thumb gusset around the curved edge from A to B. Stitch the inner seam of thumb and palm, tapering to a point at A. Cut the elastic in half. Machine-zigzag over the elastic stretched on the wrong side of the palm/thumb, 3 inches down from the top edge. Trim the excess elastic.

3 Stitch mitten palm to back along side and finger curve. Turn right side out.

4 Repeat for the lining, leaving an opening in side seam for turning.

5 Stitch ends of each cuff together. Press seams open. Fold cuff in half with wrong sides facing and matching raw edges. Baste to top edge of mitten.

6 Slip mitten into lining, matching side seams and thumb. Stitch top edge. Slip-stitch, *opposite,* opening in lining closed. Tuck lining into the mitten and turn cuff down.

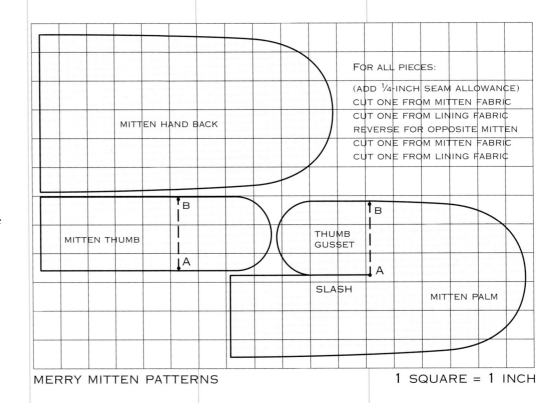

MITTEN HAND BACK

FOR ALL PIECES:

(ADD ¼-INCH SEAM ALLOWANCE)
CUT ONE FROM MITTEN FABRIC
CUT ONE FROM LINING FABRIC
REVERSE FOR OPPOSITE MITTEN
CUT ONE FROM MITTEN FABRIC
CUT ONE FROM LINING FABRIC

MITTEN THUMB

THUMB GUSSET

SLASH

MITTEN PALM

MERRY MITTEN PATTERNS   1 SQUARE = 1 INCH

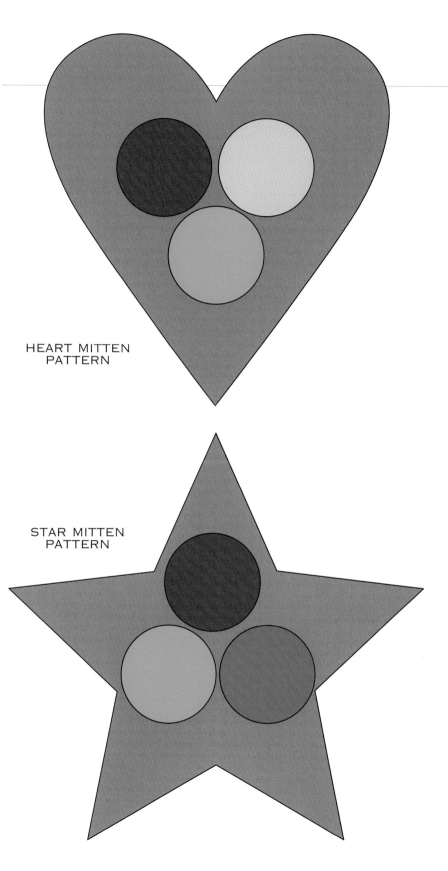

HEART MITTEN
PATTERN

STAR MITTEN
PATTERN

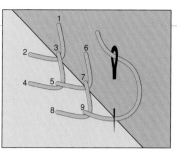

FEATHERSTITCH

FRENCH KNOT

BLANKET STITCH

LAZY DAISY STITCH

STRAIGHT STITCH

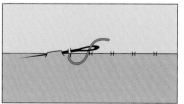

SLIP STITCH

doggy gifts

REMEMBER YOUR PERKY POOCH WITH A GOOD-DOG CARD OR A JINGLING VELVET COLLAR.

DOGGY TREAT CARDS

SUPPLIES

FOR THE DOG CARD

8½×11-inch card stock in green and white
Plaid scrapbook paper
Thick white crafts glue
Tracing paper; pencil
Scissors; fine-tip black permanent marking pen
Crayons, optional
Crafts knife
6-inch length of 1-inch-wide ribbon
1 medium dog biscuit

WHAT TO DO

1 Fold green card stock in half. Glue a smaller piece of plaid paper on the front.

2 Enlarge and trace the dog pattern onto tracing paper and cut out. Trace around the pattern on white paper. Cut out shape.

3 With black marking pen, add eyes, nose, mouth, eyebrows, and front paw outlines. If desired, let the kids color the shape.

4 Make two slits below the dog's chin with a crafts knife as indicated on the pattern. Thread the ribbon through the slits so the ends hang out behind the dog. Thread the biscuit through the ribbon loop; knot and trim the ribbon ends. Glue the dog onto the card.

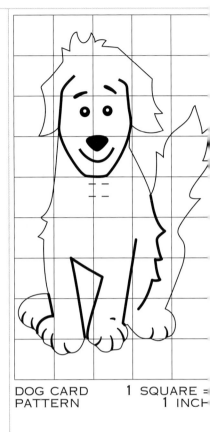

DOG CARD PATTERN   1 SQUARE = 1 INCH

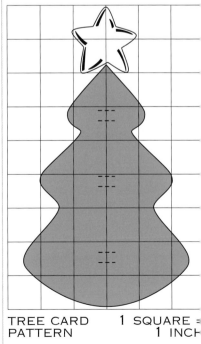

TREE CARD PATTERN   1 SQUARE = 1 INCH

through each set of slits. Tie a biscuit to each ribbon.

4 Outline the star with black. Glue the tree and star onto the card.

JINGLE BELL COLLAR

SUPPLIES

⅓ yard of blue or
  red stretch flocked
  nylon
Scissors; yardstick
Green or red jingle
  bells
½-inch-wide elastic
  long enough to fit
  around pet's neck
  (15 inches for a
  medium-size dog)
Matching thread
Needle

WHAT TO DO

1 Cut out a 9×32-inch rectangle of fabric. Stitch jingle bells randomly over the right side of the fabric. Be careful to leave an inch around the edge of the fabric clear for stitching.

2 Fold the fabric in half lengthwise, bringing the right sides together. Machine- or hand-stitch down the length of the collar through both layers of fabric to join the cut edges together. Turn the tube right side out.

3 Thread the elastic through the tube and then sew the elastic ends together. Hand-sew the tube ends together to finish the collar.

SUPPLIES

FOR THE TREE CARD

8½×11-inch card stock
  in white and green
Red decorative paper
Thick white crafts glue
Tracing paper
Pencil
Scissors
Crayons, optional
Crafts knife
¼- to ½-inch-wide
  plaid ribbon
Ruler
Small, medium, and
  large dog biscuits
Fine-tip black
  permanent marking
  pen

WHAT TO DO

1 Fold white paper in half. Glue a smaller piece of red paper onto the front.

2 Enlarge and trace the patterns onto tracing paper. Cut out. Trace around the tree on green paper and the star on white. Cut out. If desired, let the kids color the star.

3 Using a crafts knife, cut three pairs of slits down the tree center. Thread a 6-inch length of ribbon

cheery checkers

AN ELEGANT
HOLIDAY GIFT,
THIS ETCHED GAME
BOARD BECOMES
A SHOWPIECE WITH
GOLD AND BLACK
CHECKERS AND
A GOLD MESH BAG.

SUPPLIES
Scissors
1½-inch-wide
 masking tape
14×14-inch square
 of glass; newspapers
Etching cream
Paintbrush
Silicone glue
4 clear flat marbles
Checkers
Gold spray paint
6×12-inch piece of
 gold mesh fabric
Needle and thread
18 inches of cord

WHAT TO DO

1 Cut 32 pieces of
 tape, each
1½ inches square.
Press the tape squares
onto the glass in
checkerboard fashion.
Tape off a 1-inch
border around edge.

2 In a
 well-ventilated
area, cover work
surface with
newspapers. Paint
etching cream over the
exposed glass areas.
Etch glass according
to the manufacturer's
instructions. Rinse off
the etching cream with
water and remove the
tape. Wash the glass
again. Let dry. Glue a
flat marble on the
back side under each
corner of the board.

3 In a
 well-ventilated
work area, spray-paint
the red checkers gold.
Let dry.

4 Place the short
 ends of gold
mesh together. Sew
each side to make a
bag. Weave cording
through mesh 2 inches
below the top. Place
checkers in bag and
tie cord into a bow.

heart pins

CREATE MINIATURE PIECES OF ART TO GIVE WITH LOVE. THESE COLORFUL RESIN HEARTS SPARKLE WITH METALLIC PAPERS, GLASS BEADS, AND GLITTER PAINT.

SUPPLIES

Heavy black artboard
Scissors
Adhesive-back papers, such as foil, metallic, and hologram papers
Decorative-edge scissors
Pencil; waxed paper
Liquid plastic casting resin and hardener
Crafts stick; gems
Gold glitter fabric paint; fine wire
Colored beads
Hot-glue gun; glue sticks; pin backs

WHAT TO DO

1 To make several pins at one time, start with a piece of artboard as large as desired.

2 Cut the papers into small, irregular shapes. Use decorative-edge scissors to cut long strips of paper. Remove backing after cutting.

3 Arrange papers in a random pattern to cover black board, allowing small black borders to show between the pieces.

4 Draw heart shapes on paper-covered board as many times as possible. Cut out.

5 In a well-ventilated area, place waxed paper on work surface and arrange heart shapes. Mix the resin and hardener following the manufacturer's instructions. Use a crafts stick to spread a thick coat of resin on each heart. Before it begins to set, press in gems. Let hearts set overnight.

6 Outline hearts and gems with glitter paint. String beads onto fine wire. Loop ends of wire around last bead and back into strand of beads. Hot-glue onto back of heart. Curl and shape wired beads. Hot-glue pin back to back of pin.

santa sack

As a fun lunch companion or a country-style gift wrap, this merry sack is sure to please even the most discriminating St. Nick.

SUPPLIES
Tracing paper; pencil
Paper-backed fusible web; scissors
Fabric scraps in red and white; brown paper lunch sack
Paint pens in shiny white, shiny black, and iridescent glitter

WHAT TO DO

1 Enlarge and trace patterns, *below,* onto tracing paper. The dashed lines indicate the overlap. Mark the right side of each pattern piece.

2 Turn patterns, right side down, on paper side of fusible web; trace around the patterns. Cut out pieces ¼ inch outside the lines. Fuse to wrong side of fabric.

3 Cut out on traced lines; peel off paper. Position pieces on bag and fuse in place.

4 Draw squiggly eyebrows with shiny white, make dot eyes with shiny black, and outline hat and beard with iridescent glitter "stitch" lines. Let dry.

SANTA SACK PATTERN   1 SQUARE = 1 INCH

Terrific Tins

A QUICK TRIP TO THE CRAFTS STORE WILL PROVIDE YOU WITH THE MEANS TO PERSONALIZE YOUR COOKIE TINS FOR EXTRA SPECIAL GIFT GIVING THIS SEASON. WHEN THE COOKIES ARE GONE, FRIENDS AND FAMILY CAN CONTINUE TO ENJOY YOUR HANDIWORK.

SUPPLIES
Cookie tins
Spray primer
Acrylic paint in blue, purple, green, white, orange, and black
2 circular sponges
Scissors; felt in orange and yellow
Thick white crafts glue
Small pom-pom
Ribbon; small twigs
2 buttons
Snowflake rubber stamp
Spray clear coat high-shine glaze
Cotton swabs

WHAT TO DO

FOR THE SNOWMAN TIN

1 Spray the tin with primer and allow to dry. Paint two coats of blue paint on tin; let dry between coats. When dry, sponge on purple; let dry. On lid, sponge two white circles for snowman; let dry.

2 Cut out orange felt triangle for the hat and yellow strip for hatband; glue to tin. Glue pom-pom at hat's tip. Also, glue on twigs for arms and ribbon to create snowman's scarf. Glue buttons to center of large white circle. When glue has dried, paint eyes, mouth, and orange carrot nose on small circle. Stamp snowflakes around the sides of tin for trim. Let dry.

3 In a well-ventilated work area, spray the lid and base separately with clear coat. Let dry before putting the tin together.

FOR THE HANDPRINT TIN

1 Spray the tin with primer and allow to dry. Paint it a dark color and sponge on a lighter color as you did with snowman tin.

2 Coat child's hand with contrasting paint and press on lid. Use cotton swab to make border of small dots. Press thumbprints on the side rim. Let the paint dry.

3 In a well-ventilated work area, spray the lid and base separately with clear coat. Let dry before putting the tin together.

WRAP YOUR GIFTS IN HOLIDAY STYLE. A FABRIC NAPKIN, SHOELACES, AND JINGLE BELLS MAKE UNEXPECTED WRAPS. TURN THE PAGE FOR MORE IDEAS AND FOR STEP-BY-STEP INSTRUCTIONS.

NAPKIN
WRAP

SHOELACE
SURPRISE

JINGLE BELL
WRAP

To Jenny from John

to John from Jenny

NATURALLY
PRETTY
PACKAGES

NAPKIN WRAP

SUPPLIES

Cloth napkin
Water-erasable marking pen
Needle with large eye
2 yards of 15-mm ribbon
Small square gift box
Scissors
1 yard each of two coordinating ribbons

WHAT TO DO

1 On wrong side of napkin, mark center of each edge with a marking pen. Connect the marks to make a diamond as shown, *below.*

2 Thread needle with ribbon. Beginning and ending at the same edge mark, hand-sew running stitches along the drawn diamond, leaving tails of ribbon.

3 Set box on wrong side of napkin aligned with running stitches. Gather napkin around box by pulling ends of ribbon until box is enclosed. Knot ribbon and cut ends. Use coordinating ribbons to tie bow around napkin.

SHOELACE SURPRISE

SUPPLIES

Metallic shoelaces or 3 pairs of shoelaces
Wrapped package
Scissors; heavy art paper in desired color; paper punch
Rubber band

WHAT TO DO

1 *For the star wrap,* tie laces around a box. Cut a paper star and punch two holes in the center. Pull the laces through the holes; knot the ends.

2 *For the braided shoelace wrap,* braid three pairs of shoelaces together. Wrap the braid around the box. Secure it with a rubber band. Unbraid ends up to rubber band. Loop the tails through the rubber band to make a bow.

JINGLE BELL WRAP

SUPPLIES

Hot-glue gun and glue sticks
Jingle bells; ribbon

WHAT TO DO

1 Hot-glue jingle bells in a free-form design to the package top. Let the glue cool.

2 Add a knotted ribbon for an accent. Glue in place.

NATURALLY PRETTY PACKAGES

SUPPLIES

Hot-glue gun and glue sticks
Dried bay leaves
Wrapped package
Star anise seeds
2 strips of ribbon
Cinnamon sticks
Large or medium jingle bell
Wire-edge organdy ribbon
Plain cardboard box
Art paper; scissors
Gold ribbon or cord

WHAT TO DO

1 *For the wreath package,* glue bay leaves in a wreath shape to the top of a package. Add two star anise and two strips of ribbon for the bow.

2 *For the cinnamon stick package,* tie cinnamon sticks and a jingle bell together with ribbon. Glue to the top of a brown box. Cut a small slit in the top of the an art paper tag and tie short cinnamon sticks to the top of the tag with gold ribbon or cord.

NAPKIN WRAP DIAGRAM

showy soaps

If your kids like to cut dough with a cookie cutter, they'll be able to help form these Showy Soaps, a tidy package just right for the teachers on your gift list. Let the kids use their imaginations choosing shapes and colors to personalize each of their cheerful gift soaps.

SUPPLIES

Ivory soap or assorted-color glycerin soaps, cut in cubes
Bowl; spoon
Food coloring (optional)
Cookie sheet
Waxed paper
Cookie cutters
Small gift boxes
Colored tissue paper
Small sponge shapes available at crafts stores (optional)

WHAT TO DO

1 *For a basic ornamental soap shape,* place glycerin or Ivory soap cubes in a bowl and microwave on high for 30 seconds. Stir. Cook on high for another 30 seconds. Stir. If desired, add food coloring if using Ivory soap. Don't liquefy the soap. Just heat it to a goopy consistency so it can be pressed into the cookie cutters.

2 Line a cookie sheet with waxed paper. Place cookie cutters on top of waxed paper. When soap mixture is cool enough to handle, work it into cookie cutters using spoons or hands.

3 Place cookie sheet with cookie cutters in the freezer for 15 to 20 minutes. When firm, pop soaps out of cookie cutters. Put in boxes and wrap with tissue paper.

VARIATIONS

1 *For a two-shape soap,* begin with a finished shape, such as a red star. Use a small cookie cutter, such as a circle, to cut out the middle of the star. Pop out the middle shape. Then use the small cookie cutter as a mold for a soap of a different color–green, for example. Once the green circle has set, pop from mold and press into the red star.

2 *For a sponge soap,* melt glycerin soap until it is a pourable consistency. Place cookie cutters on a cookie sheet. Pour soap mixture until the cookie cutter is one-third to half full. Carefully position a sponge shape on top of the soap mixture. Pour more soap over sponge until cookie cutter is full. Place cookie sheet with cookie cutters in the freezer for 15 to 20 minutes. When firm, pop soaps out of cookie cutters. Put in boxes and wrap with tissue paper.

silver wine cozy

BEFORE GIVING
YOUR NEXT BOTTLE
OF WINE, DRESS IT
UP IN THIS
EASY-TO-MAKE
COZY FOR A MOST
ELEGANT
PRESENTATION.

SUPPLIES
Pins
Cloth napkin
Ruler
4 large decorative
  buttons
Thread to match
  napkin
Needle
1 yard coordinating
  ribbon

WHAT TO DO

1 With the right side out, pin the napkin into a tube shape around the desired bottle, overlapping the edges to fit. Remove the bottle.

Beginning 5 inches down from the top of the tube, secure the edges by sewing four buttons, evenly spaced, through both of the napkin layers.

2 Turn the tube inside out and flatten, keeping the overlapped edges centered on the side facing up. To fit the bottom of napkin to bottle, fold a 1-inch pleat on each side of tube at bottom edge. Machine-sew across bottom of tube, catching pleats in seam. Turn cozy right side out.

3 Slide the cozy onto the bottle. Tie the ribbon around cozy at the neck of the bottle.

DRILL A FEW
HOLES AND ADD
DECORATIVE
KNOBS OR PULLS
TO TRANSFORM
WOOD CHARGERS
INTO STURDY
SERVING TRAYS TO
GIVE WITH
HOLIDAY GOODIES.

SUPPLIES
Sandpaper, rag, and
  spray paint
  (optional)
Wood charger
  or plate
Pair of drawer pulls
Drill with bit
Screwdriver

WHAT TO DO
1 If a colored plate
is desired, lightly
sand the plate. Wipe
off dust. In a
well-ventilated work
area, spray-paint the
top and edge of the
plate. Let dry.

2 Decide where
to place pulls on
opposite sides of
plate. Mark areas to
be drilled.

3 Drill
holes
according to the
screw size
accompanying the
drawer pulls. Screw
the pulls into place.

charger trays

fanciful bow box

THESE BEAUTIFUL BOXES ARE A GIFT IN THEMSELVES. THE BOXES AND LIDS ARE GIVEN COATS OF TEXTURE AND COLOR AND TOPPED WITH BEADS AND BOWS.

SUPPLIES

Cardboard box with lid; pencil
Texturizing gel medium (found with painting supplies in art stores)
Paintbrush
Small comb; toothpick
Acrylic paints in metallic iridescent pink and green
Hot-glue gun and glue sticks
Ribbon
Plastic gems
Button
Fine wire; beads

WHAT TO DO

1 Place lid on box and draw a pencil line around lid onto box. Remove lid.

2 Paint texturizing gel thickly onto box. Do not apply any gel above pencil line. Use a comb or toothpick to create texture. Let dry.

3 Paint box with the desired color of paint. Let dry.

4 *For green box,* tie ribbon around the box. Tie the ends into a generous bow. Glue gems in a vertical line on the ribbon where it covers the box sides.

5 *For pink box,* stick gems to sides of box. Glue a ribbon bow on lid. Glue a button in the center of the bow.

6 String colored beads onto fine wire. Loop wire around end beads and insert back into strand of beads. Tie strands of beads onto the bow.

Sweetest

Goodies

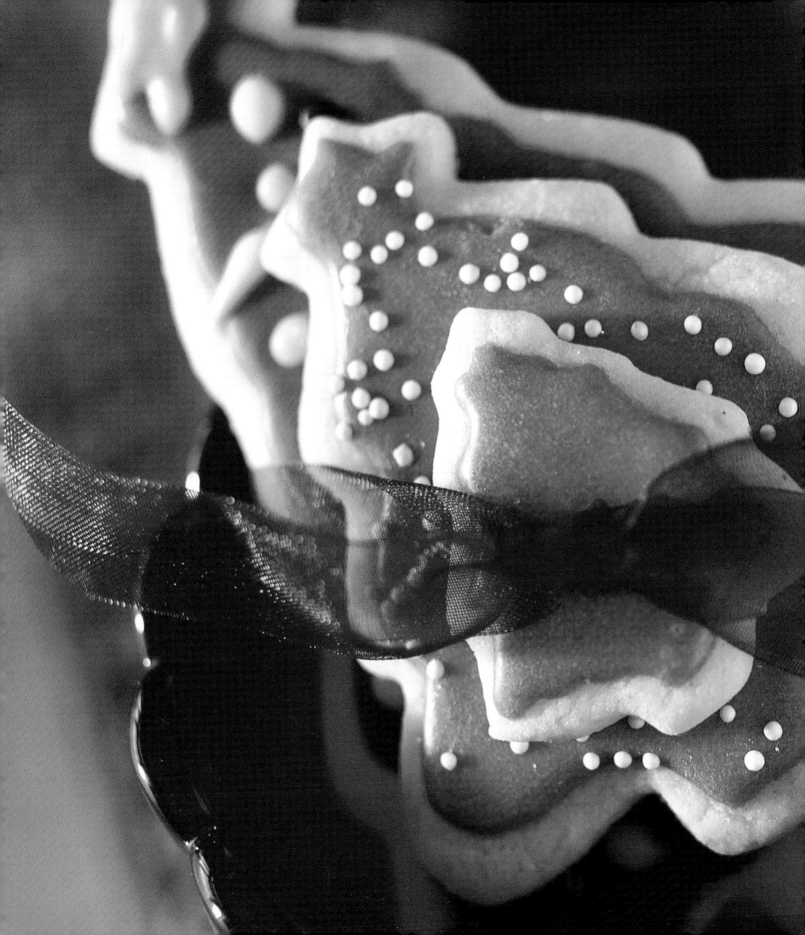

holiday tree trio

When making your favorite cutout cookies this Christmas, try using three different sizes of tree cookie cutters. After the cookies are iced and decorated, stack them in a pretty holiday bowl. Tie the arrangement with a sheer ribbon for a festive (and delicious!) presentation. These cookie temptations are perfect for party favors or as gifts for neighbors and friends who enjoy your sweet baking.

chocolate goodies

INDULGE THE CHOCOLATE LOVERS ON YOUR GIFT LIST WITH CHOCOLATE CHERRY COOKIES, *BELOW*, OR SENSATIONAL FRUITED TRUFFLES, *OPPOSITE*.

CHOCOLATE CHERRY COOKIES

SUPPLIES

1½ cups all-purpose flour
½ cup unsweetened cocoa powder
½ cup butter, softened
1 cup sugar
¼ teaspoon salt
¼ teaspoon baking powder
¼ teaspoon baking soda
1 egg
1½ teaspoons vanilla
48 undrained maraschino cherries (about one 10-ounce jar)
1 cup semisweet chocolate pieces
½ cup sweetened condensed milk

WHAT TO DO

1 Combine flour and cocoa powder in a bowl; set aside. Beat butter in a large mixing bowl with an electric mixer on medium to high speed for 30 seconds. Add sugar, salt, baking powder, and baking soda; beat until combined. Beat in egg and vanilla until combined. Gradually beat in flour mixture.

2 Shape dough into 1-inch balls; place on ungreased cookie sheet. Press down center of each ball with thumb. Drain cherries, reserving juice. Place a cherry in the center of each cookie. In a small saucepan combine the chocolate pieces and sweetened condensed milk; heat until chocolate is melted. Stir in 4 teaspoons of reserved cherry juice.

3 Spoon about 1 teaspoon of

CHOCOLATE CHERRY COOKIES

FRUITED TRUFFLES

frosting over each cherry, spreading to cover. Bake in a 350° oven about 10 minutes or until done. Place on wire rack; cool. Makes 48 cookies.

FRUITED TRUFFLES

SUPPLIES

1 6-ounce package semisweet chocolate pieces (1 cup)
2 tablespoons butter or margarine
¼ cup powdered sugar, sifted
1 tablespoon brandy

½ cup chopped toasted almonds
½ cup flaked coconut
½ cup whole pitted dates, chopped
¼ cup red candied cherries, chopped
8 ounces chocolate-flavor candy coating, melted
Cocoa powder, optional
Chocolate and/or vanilla-flavor candy coating, melted (optional)
Small gold candies (optional)
Fondant (optional)

Red food coloring (optional)

WHAT TO DO

1 Combine the chocolate pieces and butter or margarine in a microwave-safe 1-quart casserole dish. Microwave, uncovered, on high for 1 to 2 minutes or until chocolate can be stirred smooth. The chocolate will hold its shape after it starts to melt, so stir it once after a minute of heating.

2 Stir in powdered sugar and brandy. Add almonds, coconut, dates, and cherries. Shape mixture into ¾-inch balls. Refrigerate until firm. Dip in candy coating. Drop dipped truffles into foil cups or place on waxed paper until set. Decorate with cocoa powder, candy coating, gold candies, or fondant, as desired. Store in a sealed container in the refrigerator for up to 2 weeks. Makes about 40 truffles.

3 For bow, tint a small amount of purchased fondant with red food coloring. On a surface dusted with powdered sugar, roll fondant to ⅛ to ¼ inch thick. Cut into thin strips. Wrap strips around truffles. Curl small strips of fondant into a bow shape and place on tops of truffles; moisten with water to adhere.

candy delights

RESEMBLING OVERSIZE HOLIDAY PEPPERMINTS, THESE BOXES ARE PAINTED WITH SIGNATURE SWIRLS. FILL THE BOXES WITH PEPPERMINT CANDY FOR A MOST CLEVER GIFT. THE CASHEW BRITTLE, *OPPOSITE*, WILL HAVE EVERYONE SINGING YOUR PRAISES.

PEPPERMINT CANDY AND CLEVER BOXES

SUPPLIES

FOR CLEVER BOXES

Pencil; tracing paper
Round papier-mâché box with lid
Scissors
Acrylic paints in red and white
Paintbrush
Transfer paper
Tape; transparent cellophane wrapping paper
Two 18-inch pieces of 1⅝-inch-wide sheer red ribbon

WHAT TO DO

1 Trace the box lid onto tracing paper; cut out. Mark the center of the circle. Draw six curved lines to make swirls as shown in the photo, *below left*.

2 Base-coat all outside surfaces of the box lid and base with white paint. Let dry. Apply additional coats as needed for complete coverage.

3 Center the tracing paper on the box lid. Slip transfer paper between the lid and tracing paper; tape to prevent slipping. Retrace lines to transfer the pattern to the lid. Remove the papers. Use pencil to lightly extend the lines down from the top of the lid onto the sides of the lid and onto the box base.

4 Paint every other swirl on the lid and base red; let dry.

5 To wrap box so it resembles a piece of candy, cut a piece of cellophane

large enough to fit around box, allowing 6 inches on each end. Gather cellophane at ends close to box. Twist cellophane and tie a ribbon around each end.

SUPPLIES

FOR PEPPERMINT CANDY

1 pound white baking pieces or vanilla-flavored candy coating, cut up
⅓ cup finely crushed peppermint candy
2 tablespoons coarsely crushed peppermint candy

WHAT TO DO

1 Line a baking sheet with foil; set aside.

2 Heat baking pieces or candy coating in a heavy 2-quart saucepan over low heat, stirring constantly until melted and smooth. Remove from heat. Stir in the ⅓ cup finely crushed peppermint candy.

3 Pour mixture onto the prepared baking sheet, spreading to about a 10-inch circle. Sprinkle with the 2 tablespoons crushed peppermint candy. Chill about 30 minutes or until firm.

4 Use the foil to lift candy from the baking sheet; break candy into pieces. Store, tightly covered, in the refrigerator. Makes about 1¼ pounds.

BUTTERY CASHEW BRITTLE

SUPPLIES

2 cups sugar
1 cup light-colored corn syrup
½ cup water
1 cup butter
3 cups (about 12 ounces) raw cashews
1 teaspoon baking soda, sifted

WHAT TO DO

1 Combine sugar, corn syrup, and water in a 3-quart saucepan. Cook and stir until sugar dissolves. Bring to boiling; add butter and stir until butter is melted. Clip a candy thermometer to side of pan. Reduce heat to medium-low; continue boiling at a moderate, steady rate, stirring occasionally, until thermometer registers 280°, the soft-crack stage (about 35 minutes).

2 Stir in cashews; continue cooking over medium-low heat, stirring frequently until thermometer registers 300°, the hard-crack stage (10 to 15 minutes more). Remove pan from heat; remove thermometer. Quickly stir in baking soda, mixing thoroughly. Pour mixture onto 2 buttered baking sheets or 2 buttered 15×10×1-inch pans.

3 As the cashew brittle cools, stretch it out by lifting and pulling with two forks from the edges. Loosen from pans as soon as possible; pick up sections and break them into bite-size pieces. Store tightly covered. Makes about 2½ pounds (72 servings).

pinwheel cookies

LIKE THEIR WIND-DRIVEN NAMESAKES, THESE SLICE-AND-BAKE COOKIES ARE SURE TO BRING SMILES.

SUPPLIES

1 cup butter
1 cup sugar
½ teaspoon baking powder
1 egg
Peppermint extract
2⅔ cups all-purpose flour
¼ cup finely crushed peppermint candies
Red food coloring
Wood craft sticks

WHAT TO DO

1 Beat butter in a large bowl with an electric mixer on medium speed for 30 seconds. Add sugar and baking powder; beat until combined. Beat in egg and 4 drops of peppermint extract until combined. Beat in as much of the flour as possible with the mixer. Stir in remaining flour with a wood spoon.

2 Divide dough in half. To one half, add peppermint candies and red food coloring to achieve desired color; mix until combined. Leave remaining dough plain. Cover and chill 1 hour.

3 Roll each half of dough between two sheets of waxed paper into a 13×11-inch rectangle. Place peppermint dough, still between sheets of waxed paper, on a baking sheet. Place in the freezer for 15 to 20 minutes. (Leave plain dough at room temperature.) Remove from freezer. Remove top sheets of paper from both doughs. Invert peppermint dough over plain dough, aligning edges. Remove top sheet of paper. Let stand 5 minutes.

4 Roll, starting from one long side, removing bottom sheet of waxed paper as you roll. Pinch to seal. Cut roll in half crosswise. Wrap each half in waxed paper or clear plastic wrap. Chill dough 4 hours.

5 Arrange sticks 4 inches apart on lightly greased baking sheets. Remove one roll from the refrigerator; unwrap. Cut dough into ⅜-inch-thick slices. Place a slice of dough over one end of each stick so end of stick is about ½ inch from top edge of cookie slice. Bake in a 375° oven for 10 to 12 minutes or until edges are firm. Cool on cookie sheet for 1 minute. Remove and cool completely on wire racks. Repeat with remaining dough. Makes about 34.

THESE WEDGES ARE FLAVORED WITH THE CLASSIC GREEK COMBINATION OF CINNAMON, HONEY, AND WALNUTS.

SUPPLIES

1 8-ounce package cream cheese, softened
½ cup butter, softened
2 tablespoons sugar
2 tablespoons milk
2 cups all-purpose flour
⅔ cup sugar
1½ teaspoons ground cinnamon
½ cup honey
2 tablespoons lemon juice
2 cups finely chopped walnuts
Milk
1 tablespoon sugar
⅛ tablespoon ground cinnamon

WHAT TO DO

1 Beat cream cheese and butter in a bowl with an electric mixer on medium to high speed for 30 seconds. Beat in 2 tablespoons sugar and 2 tablespoons milk. Beat in as much of the flour as you can with the mixer. Stir or knead in remaining flour. Divide dough into four portions. If necessary, cover and chill for 1 to 2 hours or until easy to handle.

2 Meanwhile, combine ⅔ cup sugar, 1½ teaspoons cinnamon, the honey, and lemon juice in a bowl. Stir in walnuts; set aside.

3 Roll one portion of dough on a lightly floured surface into an 8-inch circle; carefully transfer to an ungreased cookie sheet. Spread half of the walnut mixture to within ½ inch of edges. Roll another portion of dough into an 8-inch circle. Place over the walnut-topped circle. Seal edges with a fork. Brush with milk; sprinkle with a mixture of 1 tablespoon sugar and ⅛ tablespoon cinnamon. Repeat with remaining dough and filling.

4 Bake in a 350° oven for 15 to 20 minutes or until edges start to brown. Cool on cookie sheet for 10 minutes. Cut round into 12 wedges. Transfer to wire racks; cool. Makes 24.

honey-nut wedges

delightful

DIP PINK PEPPERMINT STARS INTO MELTED CHOCOLATE AND PAIR THEM

WITH BILLOWY SNOW DROP MERINGUES FOR A LIGHT AND CRISP DUO.

SNOW DROP MERINGUES

Three additional variations follow.

SUPPLIES

2 egg whites
½ teaspoon vanilla
⅛ teaspoon cream of
  tartar
⅔ cup sugar

meringues

WHAT TO DO

1 Lightly grease a cookie sheet; set aside. Beat egg whites, vanilla, and cream of tartar in a medium bowl with an electric mixer on high speed until soft peaks form (tips curl). Add the sugar, 1 tablespoon at a time, beating until stiff, glossy peaks form (tips stand straight).

2 Drop mixture by rounded teaspoons 2 inches apart onto the cookie sheet. Bake in a 300° oven about 20 minutes or until firm and bottoms are very lightly browned. Transfer cookies to wire racks and let cool. Makes 36.

COCOA MERINGUES

Prepare as directed at left, except stir 2 tablespoons unsweetened cocoa powder into the sugar; add to egg whites as directed.

PEPPERMINT MERINGUES

Prepare as directed at left, except use ¼ teaspoon peppermint extract instead of vanilla. If desired, lightly sprinkle each meringue with finely crushed peppermint candies before baking.

SPICY MERINGUES

Prepare as directed at left, except add ¼ teaspoon ground ginger, ¼ teaspoon ground cinnamon, and a dash of ground cloves along with the vanilla and cream of tartar.

PEPPERMINT STARS

If you want to dip the stars, do it just before serving. You'll need 3 ounces semisweet chocolate and 1 tablespoon shortening. Melt together in a small saucepan, stirring frequently.

SUPPLIES

2 egg whites
½ teaspoon vanilla
¼ teaspoon cream of tartar
½ cup sugar
¼ teaspoon peppermint extract
Red food coloring (optional)

WHAT TO DO

1 Place egg whites in a medium bowl; let stand at room temperature for 30 minutes. Line two large cookie sheets with plain brown paper or foil; set aside.

2 Add vanilla and cream of tartar to egg whites. Beat with an electric mixer on medium to high speed until soft peaks form (tips curl). Gradually add sugar, 2 tablespoons at a time, beating until stiff, glossy peaks form (tips stand straight) and sugar dissolves. Quickly beat in the peppermint extract and, if desired, several drops red food coloring to tint mixture pink.

3 Using a decorating bag fitted with a large star tip, pipe cookies 1½ inches in diameter onto prepared cookie sheets. Bake in a 300° oven for 15 minutes. Turn off oven and let cookies dry in oven with door closed about 30 minutes. Remove from cookie sheets. Store in a covered container in a cool, dry place. Makes 45.

gingerbread friends

You won't be satisfied with just one of these spicy coffee-flavored cookies.

SUPPLIES

6 tablespoons butter
1/3 cup shortening
1 cup sugar
1/2 cup packed light
  brown sugar
1 egg
1/4 cup light molasses
2 tablespoons coffee
  liqueur, strong
  coffee, or milk
2 1/4 cups all-purpose
  flour
1 teaspoon baking
  soda
1 teaspoon ground
  ginger
1/2 teaspoon ground
  cinnamon
1/2 teaspoon ground
  nutmeg
1 recipe Meringue
  Frosting
Colored sugar or
  edible glitter

WHAT TO DO

1 In a large bowl, beat the butter and shortening with an electric mixer for 30 seconds.

2 Add sugar, brown sugar, and egg; beat until fluffy. Beat in molasses and coffee liqueur until combined.

3 In another bowl, stir together flour, baking soda, ginger, cinnamon, and nutmeg. Add butter mixture to flour mixture. Beat or stir until combined.

4 Divide dough in half; shape into balls. Wrap the dough; chill for several hours or until the dough is easy to handle.

5 On lightly floured surface, roll one portion at a time to 1/4 inch thickness. Cut with a 4 1/2- to 6-inch cookie cutter shaped like a gingerbread man or other shapes. Place 1 inch apart on greased cookie sheets. Bake in a 350° oven for 6 to 8 minutes or until the edges are lightly browned. Cool for 1 minute. Remove cookies to wire racks; cool.

6 Prepare Meringue Frosting. Pipe frosting decorations onto cookies. Sprinkle with colored sugar or edible glitter. Makes 12 to 18 large cookies.

MERINGUE FROSTING

In a mixing bowl, combine 1/3 cup warm water, 2 tablespoons meringue powder*, and 1 tablespoon lemon juice. Beat lightly with a fork until blended. Add 3 cups sifted powdered sugar; beat with an electric mixer on high speed until consistency of soft whipped cream (mixture won't drip from a spoon). Divide the frosting; tint with food coloring. Store tightly covered. Makes 1 1/2 cups.

Note: Look for meringue powder in stores selling cake decorating and craft supplies.

cheesecake Treasures

FRUITED
CHEESECAKE

SEASONAL SWEETS
ALWAYS PUT A
TWINKLE IN THE
EYES OF THE
BEHOLDER. ANY
ONE OF THESE
CHEESECAKES
MAKES AN
IRRESISTIBLE
HOLIDAY MEAL
FINALE.

84

TIRAMISU
CHEESECAKE

PUMPKIN SWIRL
CHEESECAKE

FRUITED CHEESECAKE

SUPPLIES

Nonstick cooking spray

3 tablespoons finely crushed vanilla wafers or graham cracker crumbs

12 ounces reduced-fat cream cheese (Neufchâtel), softened

¾ cup sugar

1 tablespoon all-purpose flour

1½ teaspoons vanilla

1 4-ounce carton refrigerated or frozen egg product, thawed (about ½ cup)

1½ teaspoons finely shredded lemon or orange peel

¾ to 1 cup peeled and sliced kiwi; halved strawberries; halved grapes; whole raspberries; and/or orange sections

Mint leaves (optional)

Lime slices, halved (optional)

WHAT TO DO

1 Coat bottom and sides of twelve 2½- or 2¾-inch muffin cups with nonstick cooking spray.

2 Sprinkle with wafers or graham crackers. Set aside.

3 In a medium bowl, beat cream cheese with an electric mixer on medium until smooth. Add sugar, flour, and vanilla. Beat on medium until fluffy.

4 Add egg product to cheese mixture, beating on low speed just until combined. Stir in lemon peel or orange peel. Divide cheese mixture evenly among the muffin cups.

5 Bake in a 325° oven about 20 minutes or until set. Cool cheesecakes in pan on a wire rack about 30 minutes or until firm. Loosen the edges of the cheesecakes and remove from muffin cups. Cover and chill for 4 to 24 hours.

6 Just before serving, arrange kiwi, strawberries, grapes, raspberries, and/or orange sections on top of each individual cheesecake. If desired, garnish cheesecakes with mint leaves and lime slices. Makes 12 servings.

TIRAMISU CHEESECAKE

SUPPLIES

¾ cup finely crushed chocolate wafers (about 15)

2 tablespoons butter or margarine, melted

6 ladyfingers, split

2 teaspoons instant espresso coffee powder

2 tablespoons brandy or milk

2 8-ounce packages cream cheese, softened

1 8-ounce carton mascarpone, softened

1 cup sugar

1 tablespoon cornstarch

1 teaspoon vanilla

3 eggs

1 8-ounce carton dairy sour cream

¼ to ½ teaspoon unsweetened cocoa powder

Shaved semisweet chocolate

WHAT TO DO

1 For crust, combine wafers and butter or margarine. Press onto the bottom of a 9-inch springform pan. Cut ladyfingers in half crosswise; line sides of pan with ladyfingers, rounded side out and cut side down. Set aside. Dissolve coffee powder in brandy.

2 For filling, beat cream cheese and mascarpone until smooth. Gradually add sugar, beating on medium to high speed until smooth. Beat in cornstarch and vanilla. Add eggs all

at once. Beat on low just until combined. Spread half of the mixture in bottom of springform pan; set aside. Stir coffee mixture into remaining cheese mixture; carefully spoon and spread over layer in pan. Place pan on a shallow baking pan on the oven rack. Bake in a 350° oven for 45 to 50 minutes or until center appears nearly set when shaken. Remove from oven. Stir sour cream; carefully spread over top of the hot cheesecake to within 1 inch of edge.

3 Remove the springform pan from baking pan. Cool on rack for 15 minutes. Use a narrow metal spatula to loosen crust from sides of pan. Cool 30 minutes. Remove sides of pan. Cool 1 hour; cover and chill at least 4 hours.

To serve, sift cocoa powder and sprinkle chocolate over top. Makes 12 to 16 servings.

PUMPKIN SWIRL CHEESECAKE

SUPPLIES

1½ **cups finely crushed gingersnaps (about 28)**
⅓ **cup butter or margarine, melted**
1 **tablespoon all-purpose flour**
2 **8-ounce packages cream cheese, softened**
⅔ **cup sugar**
3 **tablespoons all-purpose flour**
2 **teaspoons grated ginger or**
½ **teaspoon ground ginger**
1 **teaspoon vanilla**
4 **eggs**
2 **tablespoons milk**
⅔ **cup canned pumpkin**
¼ **cup packed brown sugar**

¼ **teaspoon ground cinnamon**
¼ **teaspoon ground nutmeg**

WHAT TO DO

1 For crust, combine gingersnaps, butter, and 1 tablespoon flour in a medium bowl. Press onto the bottom and about 1½ inches up the sides of an 8- or 9-inch springform pan. Set pan aside.

2 For filling, beat cream cheese in a large bowl until smooth. Add sugar, 3 tablespoons flour, ginger, and vanilla; beat on high speed until smooth. Add eggs all at once. Beat on low speed just until combined. Stir in milk. Measure 2 cups of filling; set aside. To remaining mixture add pumpkin, brown sugar, cinnamon, and nutmeg.

3 Spoon plain cheese mixture

into crust-lined springform pan. Spoon the pumpkin mixture over plain cheese mixture. Use a spatula to gently swirl mixtures. Place the springform pan on a shallow baking pan on the oven rack. Bake in a 350° oven for 50 to 55 minutes for an 8-inch pan (45 to 50 minutes for 9-inch) or until center appears nearly set when shaken.

4 Remove springform pan from baking pan. Cool on a wire rack for 15 minutes. Use a small metal spatula to loosen crust from sides of pan. Cool 30 minutes more. Remove sides of the springform pan. Cool for 1 hour; cover and chill at least 4 hours. Makes 12 to 16 servings.

A SPRINKLING OF
COARSE SUGAR ON
THIS PIE'S CRUST
SHIMMERS LIKE
GLISTENING SNOW.

cranberry-pear pie

SUPPLIES

- **1 recipe Pastry for Double-Crust Pie**
- **1 cup sugar**
- **¼ cup water**
- **4 cups thinly sliced, peeled, and cored pears**
- **2 cups cranberries**
- **3 tablespoons cornstarch**
- **¼ cup cold water**
- **½ teaspoon anise seed, crushed (optional)**
- **1 beaten egg white**
- **1 tablespoon water**
- **Coarse sugar**

WHAT TO DO

1 Prepare pastry. On a lightly floured surface, roll out half of the pastry into a circle about 12 inches in diameter. Transfer pastry to a 9-inch pie plate. Cover remaining pastry; set aside. In a large saucepan, combine 1 cup sugar and ¼ cup water. Bring to boiling, stirring to dissolve sugar; reduce heat. Simmer, uncovered, for 5 minutes. Add pears and cranberries. Return to boiling; reduce heat. Simmer fruit mixture, uncovered, over medium-high heat for 3 to 4 minutes or until cranberries pop, stirring occasionally.

2 In a small bowl, combine cornstarch and ¼ cup cold water. Stir cornstarch mixture into the cranberry mixture. Bring to boiling; reduce heat. Simmer for 2 minutes, stirring occasionally. Remove from heat and stir in anise seed, if desired.

3 Transfer cranberry mixture to the pastry-lined pie plate. Trim pastry to edge of pie plate. On a lightly floured surface, roll remaining pastry into a 12-inch circle. With a 1-inch holiday cookie cutter, cut shapes from center of pastry, reserving cutouts. Cut slits in pastry if not using cookie cutters.

4 Place pastry on filling and seal. Crimp edge as desired. Combine egg white and 1 tablespoon water; brush onto pastry. Sprinkle with coarse sugar. Top with holiday cutouts, if using. Brush cutouts with egg white mixture. To prevent overbrowning, cover the edge of the pie with foil. Bake in a 375° oven for 25 minutes. Remove foil. Bake for 30 to 35 minutes more or until the top is golden. Cool on a wire rack. Serve warm or at room temperature. Makes 8 servings.

PASTRY FOR DOUBLE-CRUST PIE

Stir together 2 cups all-purpose flour and ½ teaspoon salt. Using a pastry blender, cut in ⅔ cup shortening until pieces are size of small peas. Using 6 to 7 tablespoons total cold water, sprinkle 1 tablespoon water over mixture; toss with fork. Push to side of bowl. Repeat until all is moistened. Divide dough in half. Use immediately, or cover and chill until needed.

berry-mousse cake

A DREAM DESSERT FOR THE HOLIDAYS, THIS ELEGANT-LOOKING CAKE IS EASY TO FIX, YET OH SO RICH.

SUPPLIES

1 2-layer-size devil's food cake mix
2 2- to 2½-ounce packages chocolate mousse mix
⅔ cup cold milk
⅓ cup raspberry liqueur
1 11- to 12-ounce jar fudge topping or raspberry-fudge sauce
Fresh raspberries
1 recipe Chocolate Curls

WHAT TO DO

1 Prepare, bake, and cool the cake according to package directions, using two 9×1½-inch round pans.

2 Prepare the mousse mixes according to package directions, except use ⅔ cup cold milk and ⅓ cup raspberry liqueur for the total amount of liquid.

3 Cut each cake layer in half horizontally. Place bottom of one split layer on a serving plate. Spread a thin layer of fudge topping (about ⅓ cup) over the bottom layer. Spread about ½ cup mousse over the fudge topping. Repeat layering twice with cake, fudge topping, and mousse. Top with remaining cake layer. Frost top and sides with remaining mousse. Decorate with fresh raspberries and chocolate curls. Store in refrigerator. Makes 12 to 16 servings.

CHOCOLATE CURLS

1 Carefully draw a vegetable peeler across the broad surface of a bar of semisweet or milk chocolate. This works best if the chocolate is at room temperature.

2 Lift curls with a wood skewer to avoid making fingerprints in the chocolate. Use immediately, or place a single layer of curls in an airtight container. Cover and store in a cool, dry place at room temperature or in refrigerator for up to 1 year.

WATCH YOUR GUESTS' EYES LIGHT UP WHEN YOU PRESENT THIS TWIST ON THE TRIFLE THAT'S PERFECT FOR HOLIDAY HOSTING.

SUPPLIES

3 eggs
¼ cup sugar
2 cups milk
½ teaspoon vanilla
1 10¾-ounce frozen loaf pound cake
1 10-ounce jar orange marmalade
½ cup chopped hazelnuts (filberts) or pecans
2 to 3 tablespoons orange liqueur, rum, or apricot nectar
1 cup whipping cream
2 tablespoons powdered sugar
Candied orange peel

WHAT TO DO

1 *For custard sauce,* in a medium saucepan, beat eggs and sugar until just combined. Stir in milk. Cook and stir over medium heat until mixture just coats a metal spoon; immediately remove from heat. Stir in vanilla. Cool quickly by placing pan in ice water. Pour cooled custard into bowl. Cover surface with plastic wrap; chill.

2 Cut cake into 1-inch pieces; set aside. Heat marmalade in small saucepan until just melted; set aside.

3 Arrange half of cake pieces on bottom of 2-quart bowl or in individual dishes. Drizzle with half of the marmalade. Sprinkle with half of the chopped nuts. Sprinkle with half of the liqueur. Spoon half of the custard sauce over all. Layer with remaining cake, marmalade, nuts, liqueur, and custard sauce. Cover; chill for up to 6 hours.

4 To serve, whip cream with powdered sugar until soft peaks form (tips curl); dollop atop dessert. Garnish with candied orange peel. Makes 8 servings.

marmalade trifle

Trim The

Tree

Tree topper display

Tree toppers, vintage ornaments, and painted holly leaves are show stoppers when arranged in a clear glass bowl. Start by spraying real holly leaves with silver paint. Let the paint dry. Place a clear bowl on a silver tray. Arrange the ornaments and toppers on top of the holly, adding silver tinsel for a final sparkle.

festive floss trims

VIVID EMBROIDERY
FLOSS ENHANCES
THE SHAPES OF
PURCHASED WOOD
OR PLASTIC
ORNAMENTS. IN AN
EVENING YOU CAN
MAKE A SET FOR
YOUR TREE OR TO
GIVE AS A MUCH
APPRECIATED GIFT.

SUPPLIES

Wood or plastic
  ornaments in
  desired shapes or
  curtain rings with
  screw eyes
Paintbrush; white glue
Scissors; embroidery
  floss in red, purple,
  blue, magenta,
  orange, yellow,
  turquoise, lime
  green, deep green,
  olive green, or
  other desired colors
Wire-edge sheer
  ribbon
Large marking pen
  or dowel

WHAT TO DO

1 Apply a thin layer
   of white glue at
one end of the
ornament. Begin
winding a desired
color of floss around
the glued area.
Continue gluing and
wrapping floss around
ornament, changing
colors as you wish.
Make sure the floss
ends are glued down
securely. Let dry.

2 Tie a ribbon to
   the ornament
top, making a bow.
Smooth out the
ribbon tails. Wrap the
tails around a large
marking pen or dowel
to create curls on
the ends.

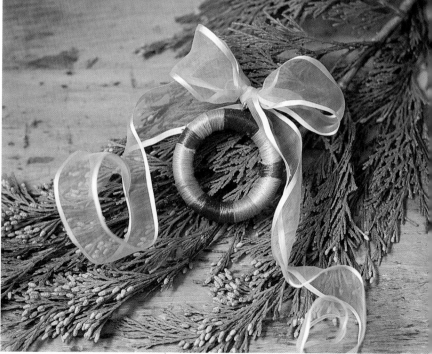

glass-bead ornaments

ENHANCED BY SHEER GREEN AND RED RIBBON BOWS, THESE BEADED BEAUTIES SPARKLE WHEN TOUCHED BY LIGHT.

SUPPLIES
Small glass rococo and seed beads
Disposable foam bowl
Thick white crafts glue
Paintbrush
Foam balls in desired sizes, such as Styrofoam
Drinking glass
Fine wire

WHAT TO DO

1 Pour an assortment of beads in the bowl, filling at least 1 inch of the bowl.

2 Paint glue on half the foam ball. Dip glue side into beads. Place the ball on a drinking glass until dry. Repeat on the other side. Let the glue dry.

3 Poke a wire into the ball. Remove wire. Add glue to the end. Poke back into the ball. Let the glue dry.

4 Make a loop in the wire end for hanging. Twist the wire to secure.

METALLIC PAINTS
AND SILVER COILS
MAKE THIS TRIM
OH SO FESTIVE.
SET IT ON A
SILVER BASE OR
INSERT A RIBBON
THROUGH THE TOP
LOOP TO HANG ON
THE TREE.

SUPPLIES

Clear glass ornament
Acrylic paints in red,
  silver, metallic gold,
  purple, and metallic
  blue-green
½-inch flat paintbrush
Lead-free solder coil
Wire cutter
Epoxy glue
Paper towel tube
Needle-nose pliers

WHAT TO DO

1 Paint ornament silver. Let it dry.

2 Paint squares of color on the ornament, letting dry between colors.

3 Wrap the ornament neck with solder and cut, leaving 2 inches at each end. Form loops on solder ends as desired. Glue in place.

4 For stand, wrap solder 1½ inches high around a paper tube. Twist the end of the solder using pliers and fold back against coils as shown, *left*.

metallic trim

candy canes for claus

SANTA WOULD
LOVE TO FIND
THESE FESTIVE
ORNAMENTS ON
HIS COOKIE PLATE
THIS CHRISTMAS.

SUPPLIES

Jingle bells in
metallic red, gold,
and green
Red metallic chenille
stems
Red candy canes in
wrappers
Thick white crafts
glue

WHAT TO DO

1 Thread four jingle
bells on a chenille
stem. Space the jingle
bells so one is near
each end and two are
in the middle.

2 Carefully wrap
the chenille
stem around the
candy cane. Glue at
each end.

A MINIATURE
VERSION OF THOSE
FOUND UNDER THE
TREE, THESE
STACKED GIFTS
MAKE AN ATTRACTIVE
STATEMENT
HANGING ON THE
BRANCHES. JINGLE
BELL BOWS ARE
PERFECT TOPPERS.

SUPPLIES

**3 miniature craft
 boxes in small,
 medium, and large
Wrapping, tissue,
 and decorative
 paper scraps
Glue stick; scissors
Thin ribbon
Small jingle bells
7-inch-long piece of
 gold cord for
 hanging**

WHAT TO DO

1 Select the combination of papers to wrap boxes. Use contrasting papers for each lid and base pair.

2 Cover the outside of the lid or base with glue stick. Place the lid top or base bottom onto the wrong side of the selected paper piece. Pull the sides of the paper up to cover the long sides of the box. Pull the paper up over the short sides of the base. Make diagonal folds at the corners as if wrapping a present. Trim off the paper ends so that only a quarter inch of excess paper remains above top edge. Fold and tuck the ends over the rim into the lid or base.

If necessary, apply a little glue to the inside of the lid or base to hold the paper in place. Continue working in this fashion until all the lids and bases are covered. Put lids on bases.

3 Stack the boxes and tie them together with a ribbon, forming ends into a bow. If desired, thread jingle bells through the ribbon ends before forming the bow. To make a hanging loop, thread one end of gold cord under the ribbon bow and then knot the ends together.

mini packages

little lady evergreen

YOUR LITTLE ANGELS WILL LOVE FINDING ALL THEIR PRETTIES (AND YOURS) USED TO DECORATE THIS SWEET AND FANCY PASTEL TREE.

SUPPLIES

Small purses
Bead necklaces
Bell and ball
  ornaments
Star wands
2-inch-wide sheer
  ribbon; tiara

WHAT TO DO

1 Arrange the purses randomly on the tree branches.

2 Drape bead necklaces from the branches.

3 Add ornaments and wands between the purses.

4 Tie a ribbon bow at the treetop. Place a tiara under the bow.

SUPPLIES

Plastic cowboy hats (available in party stores) in primary colors
Red bandannas
Plastic sheriff badges
Red and blue jump ropes
Candy canes
Purchased ornaments

WHAT TO DO

1 Tuck the hats in the branches of the tree.

2 Tie bandannas to the branches. Pin badges on the branch ends.

3 Carefully thread jump ropes through the tree branches to make garlands, crisscrossing as desired.

4 Add candy canes and purchased ornaments between the western trims.

SURPRISE YOUR FAVORITE COWPOKES WITH A CHRISTMAS TREE TO MAKE THEM SAY "YIPPEE-I-O!" DECK IT WITH COWBOY HATS, BADGES, JUMP ROPE LASSOS, AND TRADITIONAL RED BANDANNAS FOR A WESTERN TWIST. ADD CANDY CANES AND PURCHASED TRIMS, SUCH AS HORSES, TO PUT FINISHING TOUCHES ON THE TREE.

buckaroo branches

vintage images

REMEMBER LOVED ONES THIS CHRISTMAS BY TRIMMING YOUR TREE WITH TREASURED PHOTOS IN VINTAGE-LOOKING FRAMES.

SUPPLIES

Vintage family photographs or black-and-white copies; scissors
Assortment of gold and silver bracelets
Small silver or gold frames

WHAT TO DO

1 Use vintage family photos or photocopy the originals, reducing the size if necessary. Trim to fit into frames. Place photos in frames.

2 To hang, thread bracelets through open areas on the frame. Secure the clasp. If the frame does not have an opening to attach the bracelet, loop it under the back tab used to hold frame upright.

3 Hang the framed photos on the tree.

SIMILAR TO THE
ORNAMENTS OF
YESTERYEAR, THIS
ELEGANT STAR
TRIM SHINES WITH
GOLD, SILVER,
AND COPPER
TONES.

SUPPLIES
Chenille stems
Small beads in gold
  and silver
Star-shape cookie
  cutter
Fine-gauge crafts wire
Assorted gold beads
6 colored bugle beads
5-mm red bead
⅛-inch yellow ribbon
Small copper bell

WHAT TO DO

1 Thread silver beads on a chenille stem. Form the beaded stem around the cookie cutter. Twist the ends together to secure.

2 Thread gold beads on a chenille stem. Bend the beaded stem to form a circle around the star. Wire the top and bottom points to the circle, leaving 4-inch wire tails.

3 String two bugle beads and 7 to 10 small gold beads in the desired pattern onto each bottom wire tail. Bring wires together and thread a red bead over both wires.

4 Separate the bottom wires; string gold and colored beads on each wire in the established pattern until only ½ inch of wire remains. Bend ends up and poke through the second bead from the bottom.

5 Attach wire at the top for a hanging loop. Tie a bell at the top using ribbon.

beaded star ornament

THESE
LIGHTWEIGHT
PAPER TRIMS WILL
HOLD A VARIETY
OF HOLIDAY
TREASURES, SUCH
AS SMALL TRIMS
AND CANDIES.

SUPPLIES

Tracing paper
Pencil
Scissors
Decorative papers
Thick white crafts
  glue
Crafts knife
Thin gold ribbon

**WHAT
TO DO**

1 Trace the pattern, *above,* onto tracing paper and cut out. Trace around the pattern on the wrong side of the decorative paper. Cut and fold along the pattern lines.

2 Cut five triangle star points out of a contrasting decorative paper. Glue them to the wrong side of the top star points. Apply glue to the right side of the flap and then tuck it behind the first cornucopia point. With a crafts knife, cut slits below two star points on opposite sides of the cornucopia.

3 For the handle, first knot one end of a foot-long ribbon. Then thread the other end in through one slit and out through the other. Knot the end to hold the handle in place.

107

shiny trims

As radiant as the Christmas star, these holiday ornaments reflect the light with a rainbow of vibrant colors.

SEQUINED ORNAMENT

SUPPLIES

Medium-size foam ball, such as Styrofoam
Gold acrylic paint
Paintbrush
¾ yard gold ribbon
Straight pins
2 boxes jeweled straight pins with decorative end caps
Floral or corsage pins
Medium multicolor sequins; small red sequins; gold beads in various sizes
Decorative red beads

WHAT TO DO

1 Paint the foam ball gold. Let dry.

2 Wrap ribbon around the ball once; secure in place with straight pins. Wrap the ribbon around the ball in the other direction, crossing ribbons at the top and bottom of the ball. Secure with straight pins.

3 Add hanging loop with remaining ribbon; secure to top of ball with floral pin.

4 Use varying combinations of beads, sequins, and pins to trim the foam ball. Make some sequins lie flat against the ball; add larger beads in combination with sequins for a three-dimensional look. Completely cover the foam ball until the desired look is achieved.

the details of the ornament onto foil. Remove pattern and cut out ornament.

2 Place ornament on top of a magazine and use craft stick to push out the detailed colored areas as shown on the pattern. Turn ornament over to the front and trace around the dimensional areas with the pencil.

3 Color areas with felt markers. Use tube paint to outline shapes and to add dots. When dry, glue on gems.

4 Use a nail or an awl to punch a hole in the top of the ornament. Thread a piece of cord through the hole. Tie loose ends together for a loop.

CONTINUED ON PAGE 110

FOIL ORNAMENTS

SUPPLIES
Tracing paper; pencil
Scissors
Tape
Aluminum tooling foil
Magazine

Wood craft stick
Permanent felt
  markers
Gold/silver glitter
  tube paint
Plastic jewels
Craft glue
Nail or awl
Cord for hanging

WHAT TO DO

1 Enlarge and trace the desired pattern, *pages 110–111.* Cut out. Tape pattern over a piece of foil. With sharp pencil, trace around the ornament and trace all

FOIL TREE
ORNAMENT
PATTERN

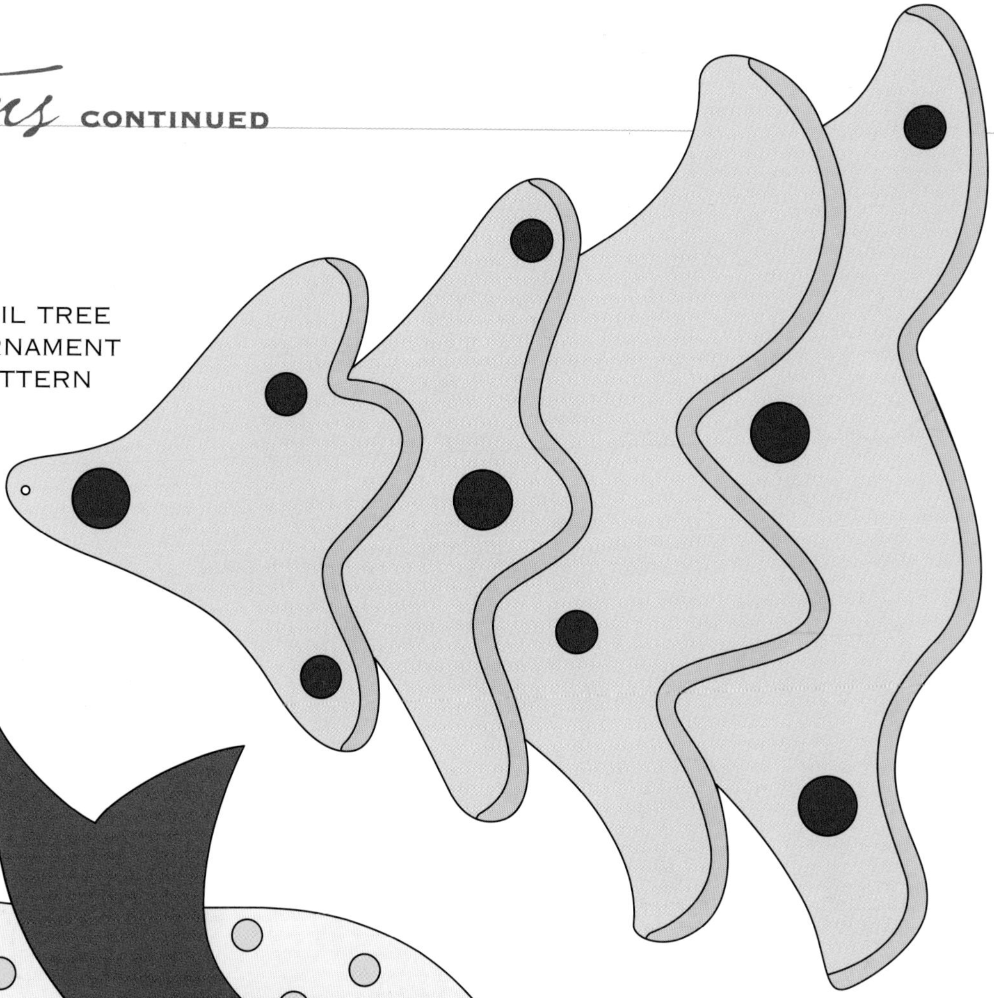

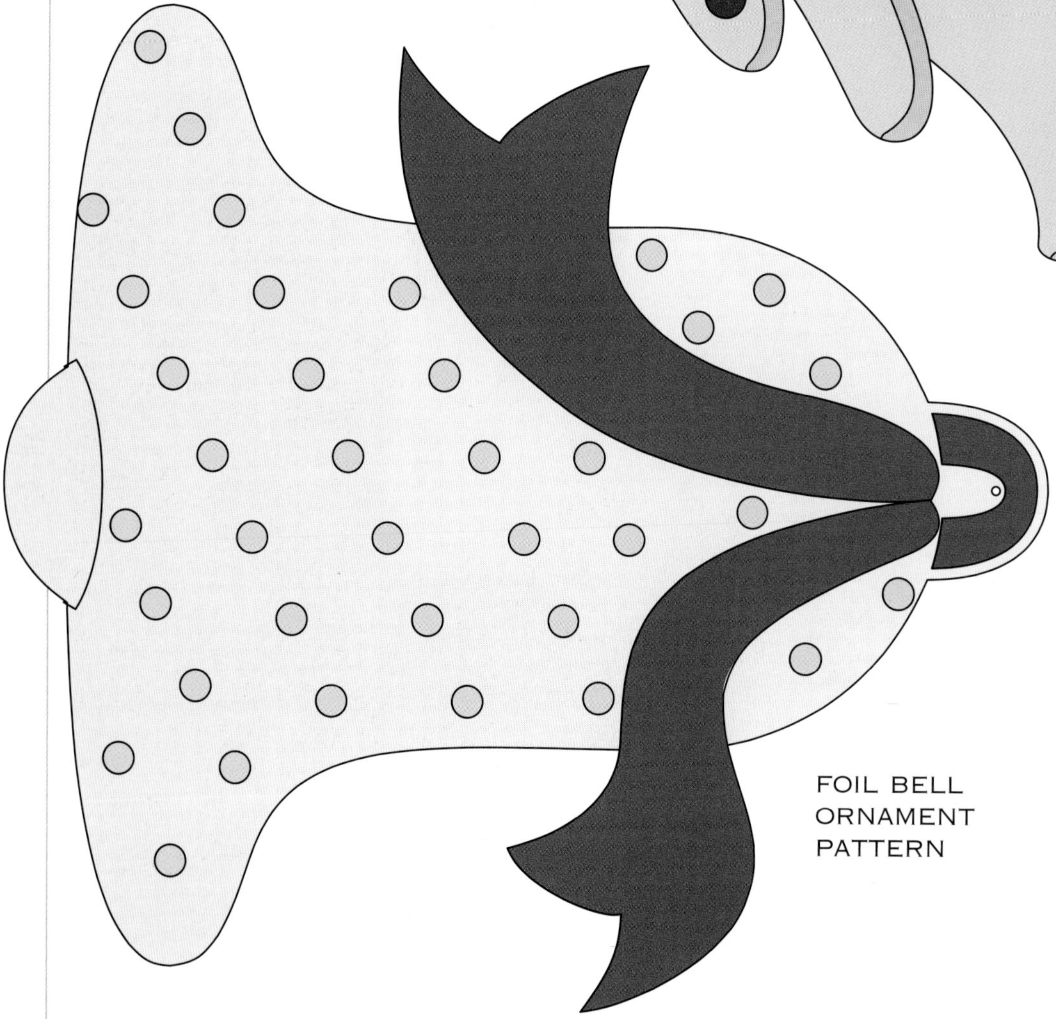

FOIL BELL
ORNAMENT
PATTERN

110

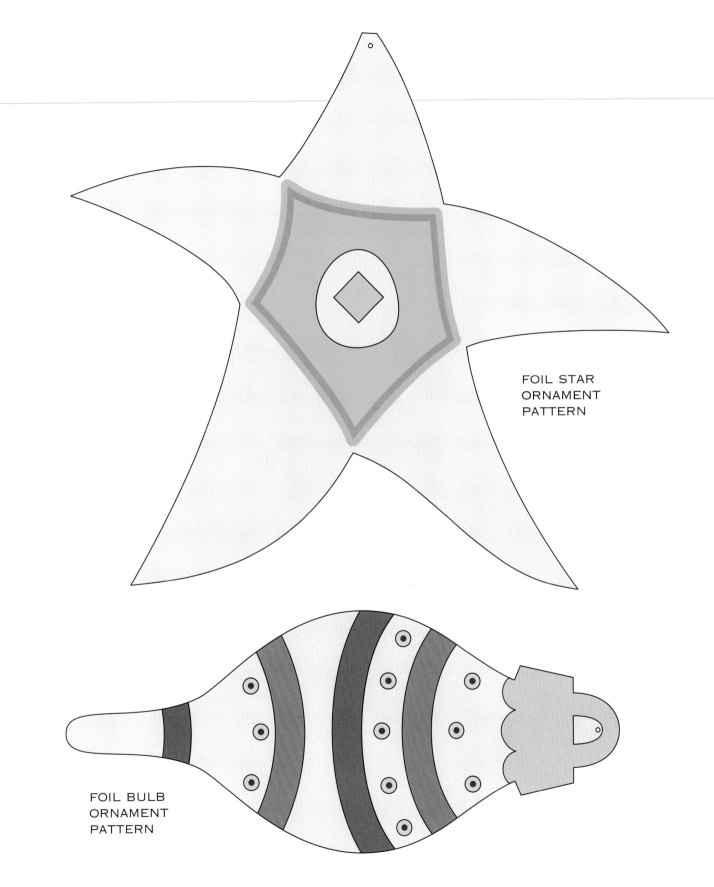

FOIL STAR
ORNAMENT
PATTERN

FOIL BULB
ORNAMENT
PATTERN

celebration stars

THESE BLUE FOAM STARS ARE SO EASY TO MAKE, THE KIDS CAN SHARE IN THE FUN. THESE DIMENSIONAL ORNAMENTS CAN BE TAKEN APART TO STORE FLAT FOR THE NEXT HOLIDAY SEASON.

SUPPLIES

Tracing paper
Pencil
Scissors
Blue crafting foam, such as Fun Foam
Silver and gold metallic paint marker
10-inch lengths of 24-gauge silver and gold wire
Glass beads in grey, white, and blue

WHAT TO DO

1 Trace the pattern, *right,* onto tracing paper and cut out. Trace around the pattern on the foam, tracing two stars for each ornament.

2 Cut out the stars and make the indicated slits. Use a paint marker to draw spirals, spots, dots, or stripes onto both sides of each star. Let the marker dry

3 Join the stars by threading the slits together. Push one end of wire through a star point and then let the star hang in the center of the wire. Push the wire ends through a bead in opposite directions to create a 3- to 4-inch loop of wire for hanging. Bend and spiral the wire ends around a pencil point.

STAR PATTERN

sew pretty tree

THIS CHEERY TREE WILL PUT EVERYONE IN A HAPPY HOLIDAY MOOD. YOU'LL HAVE FUN IN THE FABRIC STORE SHOPPING FOR THE COLORFUL CHENILLE TRIMS, BUTTONS, YARN, THREAD SPOOLS, AND BUCKLES. LOOK IN GRANDMA'S SEWING BOX FOR SPECIAL VINTAGE TRIMS.

SUPPLIES

Frosted glass ball ornaments
Assortment of chenille trims in bright colors
Scissors
Bright buttons
Hot-glue gun and glue sticks
Ruler
Thread on wood spools
Plastic belt buckles to coordinate with chenille and buttons

WHAT TO DO

1 Use uncut chenille trim, working with it directly off the spool.

2 *For the spiral ornament,* glue the chenille end just below the metal ring of the ornament. Next wrap or spiral the chenille around the ornament gluing the trim at 1-inch intervals. Cut the chenille off the spool when you're finished or when you need to change colors.

3 *For the spotted ornament,* hot-glue buttons randomly on the ornament. Hot-glue a contrasting strip of chenille around each button.

4 To finish the ornaments, cover the metal rims with chenille. Then thread a 7-inch length of chenille through each hanger and tie the ends into a bow.

5 *To make the spool ornaments,* thread on a 7-inch length of chenille and tie the ends into a bow.

6 *To make the buckle garland,* thread buckles on chenille trim or rickrack, spacing approximately 8 inches apart. For buckle trims, simply tie onto tree with loops of chenille trim.

7 *To make the topper,* cut four 16-inch lengths of desired color of chenille trim. Thread one length through a large button. Align the remaining three chenille trims with the one on the button. Tie them into a bow.

8 To add more color to the branches, tie small chenille trim bows on the branch ends.

Light

the Way

glistening goblets

Your guests will never guess that this magnificent light display was created using mismatched flea market finds. Choose glasses that coordinate, such as these with gold rims. Cluster glasses of various sizes and shapes for a delightful impact. Place a ball candle in each glass or fill three-fourths full with water to hold a floating candle. Remember...never leave a burning candle unattended.

119

A WALKWAY
DOTTED WITH ICE
LUMINARIAS
WARMLY USHERS
GUESTS INTO YOUR
HOME'S EMBRACE.
LINE A PATH OR
PLACE ONE ON
EACH SIDE OF
YOUR FRONT DOOR.
FROZEN IN
BUCKETS WITH
CITRUS SLICES,
THE LUMINARIAS
WILL LAST AS
LONG AS THE
WEATHER IS COLD.

SUPPLIES

Small plastic bucket, such as gallon ice cream bucket
Small evergreen branches
Citrus fruit slices and small bunches of grapes
Clear plastic disposable cup
Duct tape
Votive candle

WHAT TO DO

1 Line sides and bottom of bucket with greens and fruit. Place plastic cup in middle so top of cup is level with top of bucket (you may need to add extra branches beneath the cup). Continue filling in fruit and greens between cup and sides of bucket.

2 Place two pieces of duct tape at right angles across bucket opening to keep cup from floating around.

3 Fill area between bucket and cup with water.

4 Put bucket in freezer or outside until frozen. It will take 8 to 24 hours to freeze. To unmold, set bucket in sink filled with hot water to loosen. Remove duct tape and slide out ice luminaria. Cup will remain inside ice.

5 Set luminaria outside. Place candle inside cup and light. (Use small votive candles to keep flame protected from the wind.)

6 When luminarias have finally melted, pick up the cups.

Notes: For minimal cleanup after ice has melted, use only evergreen branches and food that animals can eat. Never leave burning candles unattended.

MILK CARTONS ARE THE
PERFECT MOLD FOR THESE
WHITE-AS-SNOW CHUNKY CANDLES.
USE TWO OR MORE SIZES FOR A
BOLD MANTEL DISPLAY.

milk carton candles

SUPPLIES
2½ to 3 pounds of wax and ¾ cup stearin (to make the wax burn better) or 2½ to 3 pounds of wax or wax crystals with hardener already added
Pan and a large clean can
Clean half-gallon cardboard milk carton
Broken ice
10-inch white taper candle
Superfine glitter
Large spoon
Candlemaking thermometer
Table knife
Old skillet

WHAT TO DO
1 Break the wax into chunks and place it in the can. Pour a few inches of water in the pan; then set the can of wax in the water. Bring the water to simmering and let the wax melt. (To make pouring the wax easier, you may wish to bend the can to form a spout at the top before putting in the wax.)

2 Add stearin to the melted wax. If you're using wax crystals or wax with hardener added, follow the manufacturer's instructions for melting.

3 Partially fill the milk carton with broken ice cubes. Center a taper candle in the milk carton. Tap the carton on your work surface to settle the ice. Then add more ice. Sprinkle glitter over the ice.

4 Let the wax cool to 170°. Then pour it into the carton. As the wax cools and shrinks, add more ice or wax to keep the top of the candle level.

5 After the wax hardens completely, peel the cardboard carton away from the sides. Trim the top of the taper so it's level with the top of the wax, leaving ½ inch of wick. If the bottom of the candle isn't level, slide it across an old warm skillet to smooth any rough spots.

Caution: Wax is extremely flammable. Never melt wax directly over heat or to a temperature above 220°. Never leave melting wax unattended; if it starts to smoke, remove the pan from heat immediately. If wax catches fire, smother the flame with a pan lid; don't throw water on the flame. Never leave burning candles unattended, and never burn candles where the flame might come in contact with flammable surfaces or objects.

giant icicles

Elaborate on the ice cascades that nature uses to decorate your roofline. These icicles, made with window screen and plastic wrap adorned with white lights and baubles, are as irregularly beautiful as the real thing.

Note: Consider installing your icicles early in the season so that real icicles can form between the artificial ones.

SUPPLIES

Window screen (available in rolls at hardware stores or home centers)
Scissors
Clear rhinestones, large silver sequins, and other embellishments
Boxes of plastic wrap
Strings of miniature white lights
Thin aluminum wire
Needle-nose pliers
Gloves
Hot-glue gun and glue sticks
Hammer and nails or staple gun and staples

WHAT TO DO

1 Cut screen into a long, narrow triangle. (Our icicles ranged from 15 to 36 inches long and about 8 to 14 inches across the top.) Scatter some embellishments on the screen.

2 Bunch up a long, narrow cylinder of plastic wrap; place over the embellishments along center of screen triangle. (The plastic wrap will keep the trims secure.)

3 Arrange white lights on plastic wrap, leaving both ends free at top of triangle (for stringing to other lights). Try to keep lightbulbs visible outside of plastic wrap and tuck wire within wrap.

4 Bring long edges of the triangle together and secure with pieces of small twisted wire, leaving top open. When completely wired closed, scrunch and mold to create irregular icicle appearance. Wear gloves during this step, as the screen edges and wire ends are prickly.

5 Hot-glue or wire some embellishments to outside of icicle. Hang from eaves or gutters either by wiring, nailing, or stapling. Hang one at a time, spacing as desired and connecting light strands when needed.

ICICLE PREPARATION

homemade candles

SUPPLIES

**Plastic candle mold
or food container
that can be torn
away (such as a
milk carton)**

Peanut oil; wicks

Tape; pencil; twist ties

Boil bags

**Wax crystals in white,
clear, and a variety
of colors; saucepan**

WHAT TO DO

1 Use a candle mold
or clean, dry food
carton. Wipe inside of
mold or carton with
peanut oil.

2 Position wick
in center of
mold or carton. Place
bottom of wick in
mold groove or a hole
in bottom of carton.
Tape in place.

3 Wind top of
wick around a
pencil and lay on top
of opening.

4 Pour wax
crystals into a
boil bag; secure with
a twist tie. Place bag
in saucepan
containing water and
simmer gently until
wax has melted.

5 Remove wax
from pan and
pour into mold or
carton. Let cool 8 to
10 hours; then untape
and release from mold.

*Note: Never leave
burning candles
unattended.*

VARIATIONS

1 *For objects to show
through a candle,* use
only clear wax crystals.
Pour some melted wax
into the mold. Drop
in items such as dried
fruit pieces, potpourri,
or colored wax
shapes. Pour more
melted wax over the
items until covered.

2 *For horizontal
stripe candles,*
mark off equal spaces
inside the container
with a pencil; use as a
guide for pouring
wax. Pour one color
of melted wax, such
as green; let cool for
½ hour. Alternate
colors in this manner
until mold is filled.

3 *For opaque
candles,* similar
to the look of glycerin
soap, mix a large
proportion of clear wax
crystals with a tiny
proportion of colored
wax crystals. Set mix
in a boil bag. Simmer
as in Step 4; *left.*

SUPPLIES

Tissue paper or tracing paper; tape
Lantern with glass panels
Silver glass paint
Paintbrush

WHAT TO DO

1 Draw a snowflake onto a scrap of tissue paper or tracing paper (see *pages 18* and *129* for ideas).

2 Refer to the photograph, *left,* for placement and tape the snowflake pattern to the inside of the glass.

3 Paint the snowflake on the outside of the glass with silver paint. Reposition the snowflake pattern and paint a complete or partial snowflake. Continue painting snowflakes on the glass panels until the composition is completed. Allow the paint to dry.

Note: Never leave burning candles unattended.

snowflake lantern

light toppers

Art and tissue papers transform each miniature lightbulb into an ornament. Choose from two techniques: plain white paper hats that feature Christmas cutouts or tissue paper circles that look like colorful flowers.

LIGHT HATS

SUPPLIES

White medium-weight art paper
Pencil
Scissors
Crafts knife
String of miniature white lights
Small eyelets; eyelet tool (available at fabric stores)

WHAT TO DO

1 From white paper, cut ovals 7 inches across; then cut the ovals in half crosswise. (Wrap paper shape around lightbulb to see if it's a snug fit; refine as necessary.)

2 In the middle of the half-oval, trace a pattern, on *pages 130–131,* or draw a simple design of your own. Cut out the design with a crafts knife.

3 Wrap paper shape around a bulb. Place eyelet in eyelet tool. Use eyelet tool to secure the paper shape closed. You can also use a small stapler and staples. Repeat for rest of lights in string.

TISSUE PAPER FLOWERS

SUPPLIES

Green and red tissue paper cut into 2½-inch circles
String of miniature white lights
Thick white crafts glue
No. 16 finishing washers
Pushnut bolt retainers, ⅜-inch bolt diameter (washers and bolt retainers available at hardware stores)

WHAT TO DO

1 Cut small holes in the center of tissue paper circles. Lay two circles on top of each other.

LIGHT HATS PREPARATION

TISSUE PAPER FLOWERS PREPARATION

2 Position the bolt retainer over the tissue paper hole. Glue tissue

CONTINUED ON PAGE 130

paper to curved side of bold retainer piece; let dry.

3 Slide tissue paper with bolt retainer piece over a bulb. The bolt retainer is inside the tissue paper flower, next to the bulb. Slide the washer over the bulb into the bolt retainer piece, and lock in place. Scrunch up tissue paper to look like a flower.

Note: Never leave lights burning unattended.

TREE PATTERN

SNOWFLAKE PATTERN

ADDITIONAL LIGHT HAT PATTERNS

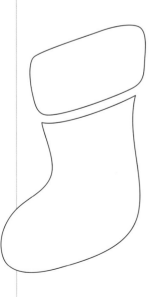

130

ADDITIONAL
LIGHT HAT
PATTERNS

antique wishes

A GLOWING REMINDER OF DAYS GONE BY, THIS VINTAGE CHEESE BOX HOLDS TAPER CANDLES NESTLED IN A BED OF PINECONES. SCOUR YOUR FAVORITE FLEA MARKET TO FIND OTHER INTERESTING CONTAINERS, SUCH AS TINS, BASKETS, AND WOOD BOWLS.

SUPPLIES
Vintage wood box
Sand
Taper candles
Pinecones

WHAT TO DO

1 Fill the box three-quarters full with sand. Arrange the taper candles in the sand as desired. Place them straight for a formal appearance or at angles for a more casual look.

2 Cover the sand by placing pinecones around the candles. Adjust the candles as necessary.

Note: Never leave burning candles unattended.

coiled candle covers

SPIRALS OF
COLOR ADD
DECORATOR FLAIR
TO WHITE TAPER
CANDLES. PLACE
IN COLORED
GLASS HOLDERS
THAT COORDINATE
WITH YOUR
HOLIDAY HUES.

SUPPLIES

**4 feet of ⅛-inch
armature wire**
**1-inch-diameter
wooden dowel**
**Blunt needle-nose
pliers**
Assorted beads
Metallic spray paint

WHAT TO DO

1 Wrap the wire
around a wood
dowel to make a coil,
leaving 6 to 8 inches
at the end. Slip the
coiled wire off the
dowel. Use pliers to
bend excess wire up
or down and then to
twist it into other
spiral shapes as
shown, *left*.

2 Spray with
metallic paint.
Let dry. If desired,
add beads or other
embellishments to the
wire ends.

*Note: Never leave
burning candles
unattended.*

SUPPLIES
Gold string
White pillar candles
Gold studs
Gold leaf
Gold-leaf adhesive
Paintbrush
Gold beads
Gold straight pins
Tassel trim

WHAT TO DO

1 *For the tall candle,* wrap with gold string. Use studs to hold the ends in place. Poke more studs randomly over the string.

2 *For short gold-leaf candle,* apply adhesive to the candle where leafing is desired. Apply gold leaf following the manufacturer's instructions.

3 *For studded-edge candle,* press studs around the top of the candle, approximately ¾ inch from the top and 1 inch apart.

4 *For zigzag candle,* pin five rows of gold beads around the candle approximately 1¼ inches apart and alternating the placement of each row as shown, *left.* Wind string in a zigzag pattern, connecting the rows of beads. Secure the string ends with pins. Hang a tassel trim from one of the beads.

Note: Never leave burning candles unattended.

TRANSFORM WHITE CANDLES INTO METALLIC SHOWPIECES WITH EASY-TO-DO TECHNIQUES THAT CAN BE DONE IN A JIFFY.

golden candles

seed-bead candles

USE ELASTIC THREAD TO MAKE SEED-BEAD BRACELETS TO TRIM CANDLES FOR THE HOLIDAYS OR OTHER SPECIAL OCCASIONS. THE BEADS CAN BE REMOVED EASILY WHEN THE HOLIDAY IS OVER.

SUPPLIES

Candles
Clear beading elastic
Scissors
Seed beads
Ruler
Straight pins

WHAT TO DO

1 To make each candle bracelet, cut a piece of elastic 4 inches larger than the candle circumference. Thread desired seed beads on the elastic, leaving 2 inches at each end.

2 Wrap the elastic around the candle and knot the elastic ends. Trim excess elastic.

3 To make a beaded bow, cut a 7-inch piece of elastic. Thread desired beads on elastic, leaving 2 inches at each end. Knot the elastic and trim the ends. Twist in the center to form two even loops. For the bow tails, cut three 4-inch-long pieces of elastic. With ends even, knot close to one end. Thread beads on elastic pieces, leaving 1 inch at each end. Knot close to the last bead on each elastic piece. Pin the bow and tails by the beaded bracelet.

Note: Never leave burning candles unattended.

yule log lights

BRING SOME OF MOTHER NATURE'S GLORY INDOORS WITH A NATURAL CANDLEHOLDER.

SPRINKLE WITH GLITTER AND WRAP WITH A BOW, AND IT'S READY TO HOLD CANDLES.

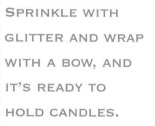

SUPPLIES

Small logs in 1-foot lengths
Drill and large bit
White glue
Paintbrush
Glitter in desired color
Wire-edge ribbon
Scissors
Taper candles

WHAT TO DO

1 On a work surface, place the log piece so that it won't roll. Mark the center top of the log. Make marks on both ends, halfway between the center and the log end. At markings, drill holes large enough to fit taper candles.

2 Paint glue on the top of the log. While wet, sprinkle with glitter. Let dry.

3 Tie a ribbon bow around the log. Trim the ribbon ends.

4 Place candles in the drilled holes.

Note: Never leave burning candles unattended.

ADD TANGY ORANGE FRAGRANCE TO THE AIR WITH THESE QUICK-TO-MAKE CANDLES.

SUPPLIES

Oranges

Knife

Serrated grapefruit spoon

Votive candles

WHAT TO DO

1 Cut a slice off the top of each orange. If necessary to balance the oranges, cut a slice off the bottoms as well.

2 Scoop out the pulp with a spoon. Press a candle into each orange.

Note: Never leave burning candles unattended.

sweet orange candles

sparkling candles

CREATE A SOFT WHITE-ON-CREAM TEXTURE ON CHUNKY CANDLES BY COMBING THROUGH DRY ACRYLIC PAINT. WHITE GLITTER AND SILVER AND GOLD METALLIC CORD ADORN THESE WINTRY CANDLES.

SUPPLIES

Masking tape
Cream-colored candles in desired sizes and shapes
White acrylic paint
Paintbrush
Fine-tooth comb
Thick white crafts glue
White glitter
Cord in silver and gold
Scissors
Straight pins

WHAT TO DO

1 Place a masking tape border around the area to be textured. Paint a light coat of paint on the area of the candle where texture is desired. Let the paint dry.

2 Use a comb to scrape the painted area in varying directions, overlapping the comb marks as shown in Photo 1, *right*.

3 Decide where glitter will be added. It can be added to the top, the bottom, in stripes, or in patterns. Paint glue where glitter is desired. Sprinkle glitter over glue as shown in Photo 2. Let the glue dry.

4 Wrap cord around the candle where desired. Cut to fit. Pin the ends in place.

Note: Never leave burning candles unattended.